FALLING INTO EASY

Meditation promotes mindfulness, presence and mental clarity – qualities sadly lacking in our stressed culture. For many of us, finding these qualities is also difficult because of the barriers our minds erect against this simple and powerful practice.

Dee Willock's *Falling Into Easy* removes the barriers gently and painlessly, leading us to hear that peaceful, small, still voice that arises from deep within to nourish us in all ways: body, mind and soul.

Dr. Gabor Maté, author of *In The Realm of Hungry Ghosts, Scattered Minds* and *When The Body Says No.*

What a concept – that meditation can be fun, natural, and something you want to do every day. Reading *Falling into Easy* is like having a conversation with a good friend who knows the path well, and walks with you awhile – to make sure you find your way. Dee Willock's gentle and insightful manner makes her the ideal companion for that journey.

Tim Ward, author of *What the Buddha Never Taught, Savage Breast*, and the forthcoming book about spiritual practice in modern life, *Zombies on Kilimanjaro.*

Despite the many proven health benefits of meditation, many people find the idea of taking up a regular discipline somewhat daunting. In this practical and highly personal book, Dee Willock demystifies meditation practice and transforms it into something accessible to all. Weaving seamlessly between philosophy, practical instruction and personal experience, she gently guides the reader through the nuances of the meditative process, along the way identifying common mental difficulties that camouflage the true self. *Falling into Easy* makes a delightful and enlightning read. Though directed primarily toward the novice meditator, the book is replete with information that will appeal as well to the most seasoned practitioner.

Dr. Michael Greenwood, author of *The Unbroken Field, Braving the Void* and *Paradox and Healing*.

Falling Into Easy presents a wise, practical approach to developing and sustaining a meditation practice. Dee Willock's book offers a fine balance of intellectual/historical references and understanding combined with creative, personal experience-based suggestions and techniques. The visualizations are excellent – poetic, calming, centering, effective for slowing and focusing the busy mind and allowing space for mindfulness and awareness to arise from within naturally. Altogether an impressive and highly useful guide to meditation, for the novice or the experienced meditator.

Ellery Littleton, author of *Old Rocks, New Streams - 64 Poems from the I Ching* and *Hummingbird Tattoo* – an award-winning collection of erotic haiku.

Falling Into Easy

Help For Those Who Can't Meditate

Falling Into Easy

Help For Those Who Can't Meditate

Dee Willock

BOOKS

Winchester, UK
Washington, USA

First published by O-Books, 2012
O-Books is an imprint of John Hunt Publishing Ltd., Laurel House, Station Approach,
Alresford, Hants, SO24 9JH, UK
office1@o-books.net
www.o-books.com

For distributor details and how to order please visit the 'Ordering' section on our website.

ISBN: 978 1 78099 026 2

A CIP catalogue record for this book is available from the British Library.

Design: Lee Nash

Printed in the UK by CPI Antony Rowe
Printed in the USA by Offset Paperback Mfrs, Inc

We operate a distinctive and ethical publishing philosophy in all
areas of our business, from our global network of authors to
production and worldwide distribution.

CONTENTS

For Serah and Maharajji

Foreword

Reading *Falling into Easy* is like having a conversation with a good friend who knows the path well and walks with you a while, just to make sure you find your way. Dee Willock's gentle and insightful manner makes her the ideal companion for a journey many of us want to take. We long for a quiet, interior place where we can pause and catch our breath – a place to re-collect ourselves, gain a fresh perspective, and then plunge back into life.

Dee's unique approach to meditation recognizes that in itself, meditating is a natural state for us humans. It's not something we have to struggle to master. It's a way of being that's available to us right here and now.

I used to take meditation very seriously, living first in a Tibetan Monastery in the Himalayas, later in a Theravada monastery in the jungles of northeastern Thailand. I also devoted considerable time to learning Tai Chi and Qigong in China. While I learned a lot from being part of these communities, there were two things I found challenging as a Westerner encountering the mystic East.

First, to get to core teachings on meditation – the stuff I found life-changing – one had to immerse oneself in an exotic culture and a foreign language. I found this to be true for most meditation traditions that come from the East, such as Buddhism, Yoga, Qigong, Sufism and Tantra, to name but a few. It's as if these amazing techniques are all wrapped up in shiny, colorful packaging. But it's the hard plastic kind that is so difficult to remove.

I've since discovered many secular Buddhist and Yoga communities in the West that approach meditation with a fresh perspective. For them, the goal is to extract from these ancient teachings the practical and transformational techniques that can be made accessible to anyone regardless of their cultural background and beliefs. "No robes, no ritual, no religion" is the motto on one such society. You can be Christian, Jewish, Muslim, Mormon, atheist, it doesn't matter. Meditation is for everyone.

The second challenge for me was the sense of elitism I found embedded in most Eastern spiritual traditions. The 'teachings' were regarded as esoteric secrets which the master would impart only to his or her chosen disciples. Or else adherents to a lineage would seclude themselves in a monastery or ashram and devote themselves to a lifetime of practice and study. The main role of the lay population was to support the monks and masters, gaining good karma for their efforts. I remember the abbot at my monastery in Thailand advising us to not speak too much with visiting villagers, because familiarity would breed a loss of reverence, and that could lead to a drop in offerings. The masters tended to treat their teachings like software companies treat their computer code. It was intellectual property that needed to be protected from outsiders.

We are fortunate indeed to live in a time in which this barrier is breaking down. The intellectual property of spiritual masters has become more like 'open-source code' – available for anyone to acquire, adapt and innovate. In the last several decades, many Eastern teachers have come to the West with an open hand, and Westerners in turn have immersed themselves in Eastern esoteric practices in order to share them as freely and widely as possible. The premium today is on accessibility – creating simple, dogma-free practices anyone can incorporate into their daily lives.

This breakthrough in accessibility in the wisdom of the East has been accompanied in the West by startling breakthroughs in brain science. Neurobiologists have discovered that the brain is much more malleable than we once believed. We not only grow new brain cells, we actually can strengthen certain neural pathways in our heads and weaken others. Our habitual thought patterns actually modify the wiring of our brain. In other words, the mind uses the brain to create itself. So when we meditate, our minds are consciously creating brain states of openness, relaxation, kindness and peace. When we spend time in these states, we strengthen these neural pathways so that in daily life they become more easily accessible to us.

I perceive this as the true and inherent value of daily meditation. For me, it's no longer an exotic, demanding practice to attain an esoteric spiritual state. Instead, it's a natural way of gently exercising the mind, so that we can easily access our deepest and most joyful sense of being.

With *Falling Into Easy*, I have indeed found it easier to effortlessly fall into these moments. Dee brings meditation into clear view so that anyone can acquire, adapt and innovate. Her book's beguiling simplicity, clarity and gentleness make it a rare gem – and something of genuine value to its readers. After reading *Falling Into Easy*, I wanted everyone else to read it and I wanted to read it again! I trust this will be your experience as well, when you walk with Dee along this path.

Tim Ward is the author of *What the Buddha Never Taught*, *Savage Breast*, and *Zombies on Kilimanjaro*.

Introduction

Meditation can be tricky and a little sticky. Just when we seem to be getting the hang of it, we somehow lose it. The very approach that worked yesterday appears to be gone today. Then when we do find our way back, and our meditation method is working, we might get a little attached to our method.

The elusive nature of meditation and the clinging nature of our minds provide us with plenty of interesting challenges. If we find that meditation seems to be slipping away from us, we can easily give up on the idea all together. Or once we find our way into the world of meditation, we might become a little stuck or attached to our approach. So what to do?

Unhinge and experiment. We can undo the claps of stickiness as though we are sliding out of a suit of armor that is binding us. We can imagine the undoing as a kind of unlearning. Instead of *learning* to meditate, we will *unlearn* to meditate. Instead of wanting to control, suppress or eliminate our racing thoughts, we will unhinge, and release from racing thoughts. We won't change what is racing, but we will strengthen what isn't racing.

Accompanying the unhinging is the experimenting. We set out to discovering something unknown, and to determine the efficacy of something previously untried. We can experiment and take our mind to new and untested places. Hey, it's our mind. Let's have our way with it. And if we bump up against some resistance, we can try to find a way in, or through, or behind the resistance. If none of this seems to be working, we can move on, and come back to that particular experiment later.

Each time we unhinge and experiment, we get closer to a meditation practice that can work for us. In the end, we may discover that meditation is not so tricky or sticky after all. Just when meditation seems impossible, we step into possible.

Chapter One

How It Started

I woke up one morning from a dream that had two prevailing messages. The first was that my car was out of oil and the second was that I should teach meditation. As I rolled over in bed pondering these messages, I felt a stabbing pain in my right wrist and remembered that I had somehow sprained it lifting boxes in the basement the night before. I got up, wrapped my wrist for the day and wondered if my car really was out of oil. When I got to my car, I realized that I couldn't lift the hood because that would require two fully- functioning hands. So I carefully and awkwardly drove to the closest gas station. When I pulled up to the pump, a service man arrived at the window with a big smile on his face, proudly displaying his nametag which read, Bud. I let Bud know about the possible oil situation. As Bud struggled to open the hood (tricky lever) I got out of the car to offer support. There we both were, leaning over the engine looking for the dipstick. As I pointed to the obscure location of the stick, Bud turned his head and looked straight at me and said, *"I'm in a lot of pain. I have had three heart surgeries and haven't found a way to handle the pain. I was thinking of trying meditation but I don't know how to do that."* Then he wiped the dipstick and said, *"You need oil all right, there is none in your engine!"* I stood still for a moment watching his face. *Did he just say that?* Then I thought, *What I should do first? Go inside and purchase a few quarts of oil, or teach him how to meditate?* I chose the latter.

I told Bud that when he got home, he should find a comfortable place to sit or lie, and just watch how he was breathing, and how his body moved as he breathed. Then he could take note of any thoughts that distracted him from his focus on the breath. If he found that some thoughts were so strong they stopped him from noticing his breath, he could write them down on a piece of paper, and then go back to noticing what his breath was doing. I told him that this watching of the breath was the first of a few steps to help him gain a little distance from the pain. Bud said with excitement that he would go right home, get his pen and paper, and really work at it. I said, *"No, don't think of this as work. See if you can find a way to make it easy, so you can look forward to it."* He nodded and said, *"Right,"* and headed off to the next car at the pump.

I thought about Bud all the way home. Bud had heard of meditation but didn't really know what it meant or how to do it. What he did know was that he wanted a way to handle his pain and find some ease in his life. And if you are like Bud, you may be holding out hope that there is some help, some way of easing out of your struggle. You may be hearing a little voice in your head telling you that there has to be another way. Well, there is help and it is close at hand. It sits just below the surface of our awareness as a kind of stillness that will reveal itself as the relief we want. It is lying in wait, only a few degrees from where we are right now. But first, let's begin by taking a closer look at the idea of meditation itself.

A New Look

The notion of meditation can be loaded with images of discipline, structure, commitment, restriction and a whole lot of shoulds. And the idea of having one more should is enough to stop us from developing a practice we can love. The thought of more hard work ahead is just too sad. And, realistically, if we were left in a quiet room with traditional meditation instructions, we would probably end up at the beach, or in front of our computers, or suddenly having to do some very important laundry. Instead, we want to somehow find a way to look forward to meditation. We hope to be saying, *I want to meditate* not *I should meditate*. We want to find a way to unhinge, to fall away and to land... and then discover the amazing richness that we suspect has been here, in us, all along. And guess what? Where we land actually ends up being just here, in this present moment.

What is the present moment exactly? Initially we see it as a concept that lies right smack in the middle of past and future: a little pocket of time that we don't often notice except when it grabs our attention. For a few seconds we are in the present moment when we step off the plane into a foreign country, or when a child is born, or when we receive a call from the doctor asking us to come in for test results. Suddenly, we take everything in, right then. We are so awake that we can almost feel the moment on the tips of our fingers as we rub them together – the moment, just as it is. Our journey now is to obtain this acute aliveness without having to travel, constantly produce children, or regularly receive shocking news.

Our journey is also about being in our world in a new way – a way that will help us sit in a place that is big enough to allow us to breathe freely and see clearly. The little voice in your head is right. There is an easier way. In this new place, we are less reactive, have less fear and anxiety, and can handle physical pain in a new way. We begin to allow layers of compassion, tolerance and quiet reflection to rise to the surface. We release the habits that keep us circling and circling the same old wagon; habits that have been with us forever. Avoidance, repression or reaction have become the norm, and have isolated us from some sort of truth we suspect is at hand. And, in this isolation, we have a tendency to dissociate from the present moment.

Escape

Many of us dissociate and disconnect. Any trauma we have experienced – big or small, childhood or recent – can make us want to escape from feelings or sensations we are experiencing. We have the tendency to leave the present moment by eating, drinking, consuming, repressing or ignoring. Or we cope with our discomfort by shielding and deflecting, as though we are holding our arms over our brows as we walk through the streets.

Shantideva, a spiritual teacher from 8th century India, describes this tendency in one of his many teachings.[1] Shantideva taught that when our life around us is uncomfortable, we feel as though we are walking around all day over hot pavement and sharp stones without any shoes on. We feel every disturbance. We are irritated by noises, smells and sights as well as conversations and opinions. We want to avoid the hot pavement and sharp stones. We want to cover over those things that disturb us. Our attempt to protect ourselves is like trying to cover everything around us with big pieces of leather – our yards, our neighborhoods, our work places, and our lives – all covered with leather so we can't feel the hot tar, the sharp stones, the critical words or the disturbing thoughts. However, Shantideva suggested instead that we cover our *feet* with leather by putting on some shoes. Simpler, I think. Working with our minds, through meditation, is like putting on a pair of shoes. We can go anywhere and experience anything and our feet (and feelings) won't get hurt. We can learn to stabilize our mind and become more solid in ourselves so people and situations do not throw us off. And as varied as our shoes are, so are our ways to work with the mind.

What We Are Looking For

Let's start by redefining the word meditation. Instead of associating meditation with lists of shoulds, we can now look at it as a kind of treasure hunt for the curious. We are hunting for some lost air space that lives in and around us and is often imperceptible. This air space sits in the gap between our thoughts. It has the ability to expand to great proportions, and send messages back to the mind about an unencumbered existence. Our mind can't figure out exactly where it is or how it exists because the air space doesn't fit any rational explanation. But we can let our minds know that it is something like white space on a page, or extra room in our closet we didn't know we had, or a secret area behind the bookshelf.

The air space can become so spacious and sublime that it defies definition. It is unburdened with the clutter of thoughts, plans, emotions and beliefs. The air inside is fresh and spacious, yet primitive and deep. This air space can propel us into glorious feelings we have rarely sensed or known.

But, we don't actually go looking for this air space, because again the mind doesn't think we have it. Instead we turn to a kind of meditation that uses the imagination to find the lost air space: a meditation that suspends the mind. Through imagery we learn to fall away from the mind's holdings and settle back into a spaciousness that already exists within us. Through imagery and metaphor, we will imagine our way through rivers, caves, teeter-totters and even a party. It'll be fun.

So now when we hear the word meditation we will know we are on a different journey – one in which we can find our kinship with Bud and let his excitement be contagious. We will give way to new ideas, and fortify our belief in this air space that has up until now escaped our radar.

How We Sit, or Not

Any meditation book, and most meditation teachers, will ask you to begin your practice with good posture. You will hear about sitting on the floor on a mat with your legs crossed and your back straight, making yourself as comfortable as possible. Or, you will learn about sitting in a chair with your feet flat on the floor and your hands resting on your thighs, palms up. Just as the Buddha sat under the Bodhi tree – the tree of enlightenment – you are encouraged to adopt this dignified and traditional position. If you are someone who has no trouble sitting like this for hours at a time, then you are off to a running start.

But for many of us, this position means discomfort and frustration, and can cause us to avoid meditation all together. Sitting perfectly straight might just be the one thing that keeps you from even trying meditation. If physical pain or discomfort distracts you, then you won't be able to stay in meditation for the long haul, and therefore won't eventually learn (ironically through meditation) not to be ruled by the pain. If you have a history of physical issues, keeping your legs in one position can cause such incredible tension that you will want to run screaming from the room. Not so conducive to a quiet meditation practice.

So, in the interest of bringing meditation to everyone, I am going to break the rules and incur the wrath of thousands of years of tradition. If you have difficulty sitting the traditional way, I suggest that you find the most comfortable position possible to begin your exploration of meditation. And I mean any position. I started out in my bed, slightly bent over a very large mound of pillows. Every few minutes I would adjust the placement of the pillows – a type of pillow art. After a while I would move to the mat on my floor and take a position that is a little like child's pose, then I would finish off with a complete flat on my back look. All the while playing a kind of homemade meditation tape that I had put together from a mix of lectures I had heard. Sounds wacky and unorthodox but it worked. I was physically comfortable enough to bypass the physical discomfort and fall easily into this new world of meditation.

The rewards have been immense, and if at all it took was a little break from tradition, then so be it. I would rather see someone, who is struggling with meditation, create a new way to meditate, instead of avoiding the whole thing all together. Customizing and then customizing again is the key to staying with meditation for the long haul. Please find positions and methods that work for you. If you do choose to lie down, falling asleep can be an issue, so be creative. Find a position that encourages you to stay with the *exercise* but doesn't lend itself to sleep. Also, don't be afraid to switch positions. You can keep your eyes slightly open to stay more alert, with your gaze slightly down. If sitting up works better for you, then do so with comfort. No matter what position you choose, try not to have your arms tightly folded into your chest. It is best to keep your arms somewhat open, so your heart is in it.

This customizing is similar to my approach to yoga. I teach that the exact physical position is not the most important aspect of yoga. I know that some yoga teachers will disagree with me but I have found that physical restriction will stop us from experiencing the essence of yoga – the union of our bodies and minds in order to know a greater wisdom. So we find a way to be comfortable in a yoga pose. Not surprisingly, giving ourselves this freedom allows for a deeper, more rewarding yoga practice.

So when it comes to a meditation practice, if sitting straight works for you then by all means do so. If sitting straight is uncomfortable but tolerable then by all means try it for awhile, knowing that you can choose to watch the discomfort as it surfaces, then quiets down, and then melts away. If sitting straight is intolerable and thus keeps you from ever trying meditation at all, then please create something new for yourself.

Finding the Time

It seems hard to find the time for a new practice. Or is it that we don't make the time? For many, the difficulty arises with the sitting posture. But when we give ourselves permission to take any position that is comfortable, what then will keep us away?

Sometimes it is our busyness. When we run around being busy, it is difficult to stop and mindfully look inward, because the running habit is powerful and familiar. Keeping on with our endless activities is a well-enforced habit. But when we do learn to stop and look inward, we will find a still, tranquil place that is worth the effort. Stopping is like waking up from a dream and realizing that we are in a different state of consciousness, one that feels okay. So instead of worrying about finding the time, let's rest assured in the belief that we will want to find the time.

When I can't seem to find the time, I go back to the basics and do what is easy. First thing in the morning before I get up, I simply try to be mindful of my body on the bed. I feel the weight of my bones against the sheet, the sensation of my skin against the pillow, and the movement of my body as I breathe. That's all – just a few seconds of noticing. A few minutes of this morning mindfulness brings great insight into how my body and breath work together. And every now and then, I give some thought to the issue of finding, or rather not finding, the time. And I will ask myself for a *different* answer for why I say, *I should meditate but I don't have the time*. What would make meditation one of those pleasures that I can't wait to do? If we think of the small comforts we grant ourselves, the ones that allow our shoulders to drop and our breath to melt, then we might come up with a new answer. Whether it is taking a hot bath, walking in the woods or sinking back into an old armchair, we need to get a clear picture of what it is that allows us to let go, and then what kind of meditation would allow us to do so. As we progress through this book we will be developing a meditation practice that so resembles comfort and relief, that we will be eager to *practice*.

What We Are Talking About

So far, I have used words such as meditation, mindfulness and present moment. Let's simplify these terms. Meditation is about calming the mind, finding an inner stillness and peace, and achieving clearer states of awareness. Mindfulness can be described as an acute awareness of our present moment or action. To meditate is to be mindful and to be mindful is to meditate. They are both about being present, being focused and being aware of what is going on right now at this time, on this day, in this present moment. When we are mindful, we have full awareness of each step, each breath and each touch. Mindfulness

brings us into our body where we can have a physical understanding of awareness. We lift the cup, button our coat and touch
the door handle, all with deep seeing and feeling, knowing each
sensation and movement. If we think of a first kiss we know
mindfulness. We know and remember sensation, touch and
warmth. We find our way to acute awareness of our lives through
meditation. And through meditation we find a quiet that allows
for mindfulness. Through mindfulness we find a sweet acceptance of what is right in front of us.

The Unexpected

Something special can occur in this meditation process we are
about to undertake together. In fact, unusual things occur in your
world whenever you change your mind. You begin to see people
and situations differently. You don't react in the habitual ways.
Even better, this change is a bit of a quick fix that falls into your
lap when you're not looking, and when you're not struggling.
Okay so quick fix is a tricky phrase but you do actually learn to
settle into an easier place without taking years off your life. What
you will come to understand is that if you undertake this
meditation thing with no great expectations, the unexpected
magically begins to happen.

One More Thing

Earlier I talked about how the words discipline, structure and
commitment can send us running from the room. So let's look at
these in a new way. Maybe our commitment now is just to show
up. No big agenda, no big expectation. Just show up day after
day as though we were sitting in a boat that was on automatic
pilot. Our boat holds its course through storms and wind, and
clear skies alike. The only discipline we need right now is to tap
into our willingness to show up, sit in the boat, and get quiet. We
don't show up to work. We just show up and start watching.

Chapter Two

Watching

So here we are about to take our first step, and we may have some old voices finding their way back to us. They might be saying,

- *Meditation is boring.*
- *I can't make my thoughts go away.*
- *My friends can meditate but I can't.*
- *I don't like the present moment.*
- *It hurts to sit still.*
- *If I just watch my breath I'll fall asleep.*
- *I need my busy mind in order to succeed.*
- *New age words make me resist all of this.*
- *What about my happy thoughts?*
- *I like thinking about the past and the future.*

Okay, so let's decide for now *not* to meditate, *not* to try to be in the present moment. We can breathe a sigh of relief because we are not going to try to do anything. Instead, we start with what's easy. We start to watch, just watch.

Watching the Breath

We start by watching the breath. You may say, *Really? This again?* Yes, the breath idea seems trite and overdone but there is something here, so stay with me. We won't be watching the breath in the usual way. We will simply be noticing how the body moves as we breathe. Somehow, something somewhere is moving as we breathe. What moves? What doesn't move? What expands? What doesn't? How does air feel when it moves in us?

How does breath sound? How *does* air move in and out? Watching and noticing.

Then suddenly we lose the focus. We have no idea what is happening with the breath because thinking has arrived unbidden. After only a few seconds our mind has taken off in ten different directions and at lightning speed. Thoughts are every-where and they seem to be out of control. Busy-mind, sometimes called monkey-mind, is running the show. Thoughts running rampant have become our norm. Darting from one idea to the next has become habitual. So now we watch the darting and the running rampant. How fast are my thoughts going? How many thoughts can I have in only a few seconds? Simply take stock. This is a pivotal moment, because we have made a choice to recognize thinking and then to go back to a single focus. We have really seen and accepted our busy mind, and we decide to gingerly go back to watching the breath.

Pretending

But now we try watching the breath from a new angle. We try imagining or *pretending* that staying focused on the breath is easy (big stretch) – as though we have been doing this forever. We act our way through this. We *pretend* that we *can* focus on body movements as we breathe, and that we *can* feel and hear air moving through us as we breathe in and out. Just acting as though we are long-time breath watchers shifts our experience. Now we can easily feel cool air expanding our lungs as we inhale, and warm air falling from our body as we exhale. As we go through this *pretending* exercise, we realize that we are able to stay a little more focused, even if only for a few seconds. But for those few glorious seconds, we slipped into quietness, we unhinged from the mind's business and had a break from thinking – a complete break. How liberating.

Those few seconds of quiet mind will leave us wanting more. In our excitement to have more, we may sense a new determination arising. This is helpful, and then not so helpful. Helpful because we are motivated to find a sense of relief again through this unhinging, but risky because this is exactly the point when we unknowingly start to push and create tension. We think we can push thoughts away to get to that quiet place again, to be free from so much thinking. So we push in order to feel free – big problem. Pushing closes the air space we are trying to get to. Pushing leads to compression, and the new air space is all about expansion. Identifying the sensation of pushing is key. Once we recognize a push, we say *Okay, that feels like pushing, so I am going to unhinge again*. We are going to learn how not to push, shove or resist thoughts, by finding creative ways to unhinge and then unhinge again.

Dissection

Unhinging can happen by seeing what is true. So we turn around and look directly at our busy mind. We go back to watching. Which thoughts are strong and which are mild? Which dominate our mind and which rest nonchalantly on the sidelines? It is helpful to label the thoughts: work, family, money, health, ideas, plans, and so on. Then look at how they appear in your mind. Are they always images, or are they sometimes displayed as words written across a kind of screen? Are there mixes of past and future thoughts, or does one time frame dominate? This is the dissection phase in which you look very closely at what occupies your mind, for probably 95 percent of your waking hours.

We have heard that we can get lost in thought, so we watch how our thoughts *can* take us over. We have heard that thought patterns are cyclical so we take a closer look. We watch how they move, how they change, and in how many directions they veer. We watch, listen and learn. The images, feelings and ideas produced by our thoughts will vary from person to person. But there are common themes. We repeat scenarios of past events.

Why did that happen to me? or *How could that have been different?* or *If I had only said this, then that wouldn't have happened.* Or we run a tape of how the next few days will go, *I am anticipating that so-in-so will react this way.* Or *I can imagine how that will turn out!* We keep playing the same tapes, and thinking about past and future events in the same way. These thinking habits are well-defined – born out of ideas and behaviors that are regularly repeated and tend to occur subconsciously. But if we can increase our awareness of these thinking habits, we can begin to witness them rather than be entangled by them. Instead of being run ragged by the monkey-mind, we watch.

We watch everything that we feel, sense, smell, taste, think and worry about. We might be thinking about a conflict at work. First we run through the events that brought on the conflict, then what we said to a co-worker, and then what we wish we had said instead. These three aspects of the issue will run through our mind endlessly. But a new perspective on our conflict begins to emerge as we watch. The replaying of the scene begins to change shape and texture. We as the witness begin the process of differentiating ourselves from the conflict. Entanglement eases and curiosity emerges.

Thought Trails

In addition to cyclical thought patterns, we experience thought trails running off in indiscriminate directions. A thought trail from my repertoire looks like this: I was watching my breath, and I heard a crow cawing outside my window. The crow sound reminded me of the tropical birds in Mexico. Mexico made me think of La Manzanilla, a small town I visited with my family last year. In La Manzanilla, we checked out an art studio. My mom loved the art, and she thought of getting back into painting. I thought of how my mom had also wanted to go back to Ontario to visit her brother. Her brother's farm was a haven for us kids when we were young. I thought of those hot summer days riding horses in the back fields. I remember falling off and bruising my tailbone. I thought of my sore back these days and how I had forgotten to write down my next chiropractic appointment. Then I remembered that the chiropractor had moved to a new office. I wondered about parking at the new office. Parking made me think of my car which needed an oil change. Oil made me think of the olive oil marinade I had sitting on the counter. Would the cat start licking it? Worrying about what the cat was doing right then, I *woke up*.

But incredibly my mind would not have needed all of these words to speed through this trail. It would have been more like this: breath, bird, Mexico, town, art, mom, Ontario, farm, horse, back, appointment, parking, car, oil, and cat – and all at lightning speed.

The point here is not to dwell too much on the details but instead to recognize how quickly we get derailed from watching the breath. It is helpful at this point to take a look back at what just happened. So, after I verified that the cat was not in fact eating the marinade, I sat down and started tracing back over the trail of thoughts to see how I got so far off track. When we do this, we can pinpoint the first few thoughts that took us away. Detecting the first few distractions eventually allows us to catch the derailment earlier. We do this by being keenly aware of the consistent derailing thoughts. For me they seem to be of the same nature and usually have to do with sounds in the room, which will remind me of some event. Sometimes, though, it is a sensation that catches me. I would be watching my breath and my back would suddenly get very itchy. Then the itchiness made me think of the new cream I had just bought at the health store. Then the store made me think of… and I was off and running.

Derailment

To increase your awareness of the derailment, you can immediately pay attention to the first thought that takes you away. If, like me, a sound grabs your attention, notice what idea or associ-ation you have with that sound, and see what your mind wants to do with the idea. Then ever so gently you bring your focus back to the breath the next time you hear that sound. You can watch this and see if there is a pattern of initial distractions. Whether it is a sound or a sensation or a random notion that has landed out of nowhere, we are easily taken away by the mind.

Looping Back

Sometimes I like to see where exactly my mind wants me to go. I pick a sound in the room that *could* easily be a distraction – the kind that automatically leads to a thought trail. Or I pick a belief that I know runs my life, even on a good day – one that sets me up for a string of related beliefs. I watch to see how my initial distraction, whether sound or belief, encourages a leap to the next distraction which leads to the next, and then I see that I am off and running again. But I try not to let this fiasco go on for too long. Otherwise, I lose my awareness of what I'm doing and I am lost in thought again. I like to stop the unintentional wandering off after four or five *thought leaps*, and then trace the trail back. For example, I might listen for the sound of the bird, then let my mind go to the thought of Mexico, then the town, then the art and then… Whoa, back it up! Tracing back helps me see that art came from town, town came from Mexico, Mexico came from bird and bird came from sound. Okay, I'm back. I'm back to watching the breath.

This tactic gives us an appreciation of the power and scope of the wandering mind, and a clear understanding of a pattern of initial distraction. Identifying the point where the mind first takes off is key. For example, the cawing of the crow pulled me away in an instant. And if I become very familiar with that split-second distraction, I can much more easily catch it the next time around. So, when I am watching my breath and I hear the crow cry out, I look for the smallest and barely perceptible manifestation of a thought trail. Just the awareness of a potential thought trail gets me back on track

While all of this watching is going on, you might become frustrated with the seemingly slow and prodding nature of learning to meditate. No worries, slow is actually fast. Slow deepens our understanding of how the mind behaves. So apply patience and create a sense of ease as you go. Instead of being frustrated by how easily you are derailed, become curious and mindful. Just as I advised Bud, avoid making the exercise seem like work. You can ask yourself what would make the process of watching the breath easier. What would make you look forward to delving into the world of meditation? If you apply curiosity and a neutral inquisitiveness, you will want to keep going and learning.

Watching the breath gets easier when we see what the breath offers. After years of meditating, I have come to understand the hidden opportunity in the breath. It is the consistent one. The breath is always there, no matter what, and it provides a profound steadiness that we can tap into anytime. In a way, the breath actually is meditating for us all the time. We are *being breathed* by the air moving in and out of our bodies. The breath takes on a life of its own. *It* has the constant focus and the commitment that we might lack. *It* is the *sweet return* that comes back to us over and over again.

This layer of consistency, called breath, sits just underneath our awareness at all times. And just as reliable as our breath is, to come back over and over again, so too is our ability to come back to watching over and over again. The breath symbolizes our inherent steadiness and our basic life force. The breath rolls in and out like the eternal wave, and we ride on this wave consciously (when mindful) and unconsciously (when asleep). We can ride the wave anytime, and if we fall off we just catch the wave, the next time around.

Present Moment

Watching the breath is about being right here, right now, in this present moment. But what can be happening, in this present moment, is that our mind is anywhere *but* the present moment. The mind is both used to and eager to wander off and fantasize about the future, ruminate about the past, and repeat familiar thought scenarios. In our efforts to come back to the present moment, and watch the breath, we attempt to get rid of the pervasive thoughts. To get rid of them, we push at them. And if they won't go away, we just try harder, and, before we know it, tension is back.

Tension comes from resisting what is. If we think that we need to get rid of thoughts or that thoughts are bad, we will push against them or try to repress them. Any slight resistance of thoughts will create tension in the body and will take us right back to thinking more thoughts – this time we'll be thinking about getting rid of thoughts! As soon as we push or repress, even slightly, we create tension. The tension can be obvious, once we are aware of it, or it can escape us entirely.

Our determination to *get it right*, stay with the breath and keep focused can cause us to tighten or push. Sometimes our attempt to quiet the busy-mind can be so subtle that it is almost imperceptible. The pushing away can be as light as resting your hand on a pillow, or focusing your eyes in the early morning. You can barely feel the weight of your hand, or the pull in your eyes but it is there. In turn, you can barely feel the push and determination to stay with the breath. Yet the tension can be there, and the push against something then implies that the something is bad or it is something we don't want. Then we get judgment. But thoughts aren't inherently bad. It is just that we inadvertently allow them to distract us, consume us or enrage us. We can end up following the endless trail of thoughts that go on forever, with no rest in sight. In our effort to not be so ruled by thoughts we push at them. But instead we just want to watch thoughts, not annihilate them.

Push Versus No Push

So how do we detect this barely perceptible push? Are we forcing our thoughts to retreat so we can focus on the breath? Yes, probably we are. The subtle sensation of our hand on the pillow, or the slight pull in our eyes, as we focus tells us where to begin. When we release our hand or close our eyes, we notice the barely perceptible sensation of not pushing. Then we repeat the hand and eye movements, and again notice the push. We repeat these push and non-push exercises. In so doing, we reinforce our perception of the subtle difference between tension and non-tension. And as we release from tension, we begin to notice a spacious feeling in our body, as if more air can suddenly find its way through us. Feeling the slight nuances of breathing, pushing, non-pushing and watching will take us far.

And, of course, as we watch, our mind wants to put in its two cents. So we listen and then create a way to dissolve the resistant voices such as, *This is dumb. This won't work.* We choose to suspend judgment and trust in the simpler process of not trying. We wait for a spacious place to open up, and we do nothing but watch the breath and wait. What is this spacious place? Again, we suspend judgment on any of these words. We go back, reduce our intent down to just watching the breath and watching ourselves watching the breath. We can't imagine how any kind of profound experience can emerge from doing so little. We don't even know what to expect, or if a profound experience will occur. Again, we stop thinking about outcomes. We commit again to just following the *sweet return* back to where it started. If we can get to a place of stillness, then the unexpected starts to happen. This is the stillness that rings true for us, as though we have known this place all along.

In this stillness, we sit with what is true. And what is true may be that we have feelings of deep sadness or residual anger. These emotions may now want to surface. See if you can let them rise without getting tense or frightened. Watching our emotions rise and fall is just like watching the breath rise and fall. Our emotions are part of our humanness. By simply watching, we are increasing our capacity to recognize and accept, without judgment, what is within us. Our deep emotions and our distracting thoughts are all part of the human condition. And if feeling strong emotions just starts to feel like too much, no worries, thoughts are right there, ready to rush in and save the day. Distracting thoughts can take over in no time. So then we go back to watching the distracting thoughts, trying not to get too caught up in their judgments. Then, we go back to watching the breath and so on.

Holding On

Suspending judgment about thoughts can be tricky and somewhat sticky. If we take a close look at them, we can see which are more tenacious then others. As we watch thoughts, we will find that some are rather weak and fleeting while others are strong and determined to attach themselves to us. Some are barely perceptible, while others catch our attention and won't let go. The Tibetan word *shenpa*[2] signifies the level of attachment to, or identification with, a particular thought, idea or situation. Pema Chodron, a Buddhist nun and Director of Gampo Abbey in Nova Scotia, has been a great inspiration in my studies of meditation, and she helped me to understand the many faces of *shenpa*. We can experience strong *shenpa* with some thoughts and not much *shenpa* with other thoughts. If a thought only distracts us slightly, then it is said to have only a little *shenpa*. If a thought has a lot of power and wants to hold on tight, then it is said to have a lot of *shenpa*. A lot of *shenpa* means a lot of reaction and investment in the thought or idea. Strong *shenpa* thoughts cling to us, as if they are holding on for their lives. They demand that we take notice, and we may be stuck with them for some time.

Strong *shenpa* can feel like a shockwave running through us. Our whole body reacts and tightens. If we suddenly remember an argument with a partner, or a conflict at work, or an unresolved issue, we will feel the catch, the *shenpa*, and the tension in the body. The Western equivalent would be having our buttons pushed. When *shenpa* is strong, our gut reaction is to tighten. Every time we tighten we strengthen the habit of tightening, and around and around we go, reacting the same way over and over again. Meditation can help with this, and watching is the first step.

The moment that we are aware that we were caught by some strong *shenpa* is when the unhinging needs to begin. Just seeing and recognizing *shenpa* begins the unhinging process. And if we are so caught that recognition is not enough, we go back to writing down the thoughts that won't unhinge. Putting strong *shenpa* on paper diffuses it a little. Then as difficult as this may sound, we go back to watching. What is happening right here, right now, in this present moment? The parade of wandering thoughts continues, and we just watch, and the *shenpa* begins to soften.

Visualizations

Tenacious thoughts remind us of children waving their arms in the air trying to get our attention. Visualizing how these thoughts behave helps us to understand what we are dealing with, and to empathize with our struggling minds. Through visual images, we can begin to let go of sticky *shenpa* and persistent thought patterns. We approach visualization with an open mind and trust that our imaginations can take us much further than we know. It can help us give way to not knowing. It can take us directly to the unexpected. Through these next visualizations, we will leave literal meaning behind and allow ourselves to fall into images and sensations. But here comes the tricky part. Some words can have a past. Some words and images have been used so much that we can be numb to them or find them too corny or overdone. The wind howling, the river running, or the breath moving like a wave have all been used many times. When hearing them, our mind chatter may move in and say, *too cliché, too poetic or too pretty*. If this happens, then the imagery is lost. Our mind says that we are not going to experience anything new here, so let's move on.

But wait. Can we find the willingness to suspend all previous connotations of these words, so we don't fall short of the experience? Can we see these words as just two-dimensional lines and symbols lying on a page? If we can, then maybe these words, in their raw form, could elicit a new response. If we decide to look at the words from a different angle, then a different association may appear. Perhaps, we can lift ourselves up over the piles of lines and symbols, up where the air is fresh, and see something new. We can *decide* to breathe new meaning into these consonants and vowels. With that decision made, we can then slide back down into the words and their images, as if for the first time. *Acute, alive* and *vibrant* replace *been there, done that*. The old, *I have heard this before*, turns into, *that's interesting*, or *that's different*, as we make these images our own. Keep in mind that it is our choice at any moment to make this turn, and to shift our attitude.

As you read this first visualization, take a pause between each stanza to close your eyes and imagine. Then as you read on, let the words wash over you and your imagination carry you.

River

Sitting on the soft, grassy bank of the river
You watch the movement of water
And the sway of the current
As you breathe

Feel the river's rhythm
Take you over

Feel your body
Begin to rise and fall
Moving like river water
Fluid and easy
Water rising as you breathe in
Falling as you breathe out
Your body becomes the river

The river becomes your body
Your breath moves the water
The water moves your breath
You take on the sound
The smell and the feel
Of moving water
Fluid and easy
Rocking and swaying

Let the movement of the river
Live inside you
Washing away you the person
The thinker, the believer
Washing all of it downstream
Further and further
Washing away thoughts
Leaving just water
River rising
River falling

But some thoughts stay
They won't be washed away
They cling to rocks
And wrap themselves around branches
They hold on tight
Wanting to be seen and heard

But when you look in their direction
They finally give way
Releasing their grip
Moving with the water
Moving with your breath

And what thoughts are left?
Which ones hold on?
They are the strong ones
The bold ones
The ones that say... I am real
They are afraid to go
They are afraid of the water
You offer a way out, a way to stay afloat
You send them downstream
Some on rafts, some in small boats
Carried down the river
Riding on the breath
Safe and comfortable... off they go

And you are back again
Returning to breath
Returning to water
River rising
River falling
Fluid and easy
The river is all you
The breath is all you
Just breath, just water

Keep noticing the rhythmic movement of your breath as you read on, and always remember that there is something to experience here that goes way beyond where thoughts and ideas can go.

I'd Rather Be

When we have an experience that is outside our usual thought patterns, we develop new ways to manage our minds. We can be deep into some futile thoughts that are running us ragged and we simply say *enough*. No fanfare, no big explosion, just *enough*. It's time for peace. We say to ourselves, *I'd rather be. I'd rather be connected to breath. I'd rather be feeling quiet. I'd rather be experiencing more room in my head and my body. I'd rather be with what is.* We say the phrase, *I'd rather be*, over and over again; *I'd rather be* is such a simple phrase but it holds so much power. The phrase represents your ability to make a clear decision. That's all. You are saying that you would rather be over there watching the breath. Then your mind says, *Well then, if you would rather be doing that, then go ahead.* This mind stuff is wide open to very creative play.

It Just Is

We develop neutrality by standing in the center of our life and seeing what is above us, below us, ahead of us and behind us. This positioning is a metaphor for watching and it allows us to disengage and just watch. When a thought arises we see how much *shenpa* it has. We can even give a number value to the amount of *shenpa* we feel. Then when the next thought arises we assess it in the same way. If one thought has a strong pull and another has a weaker pull, we can try switching them around and assigning the strong pull to the weak thought and the weak pull to the strong thought. Then we see how interchangeable they are. Hey, it's our mind; we can do whatever we want. As we watch and assess, we are disengaging, but not repressing. This is a key distinction. Disengaging or differentiating is about bringing in the slightest bit of breathing space between mind and self. What captures us in our mind is different than the self that is watching the mind. This differentiation allows us to see what is true. We are not making anything wrong or anything particularly right.

Observation can get off track sometimes. But the mind often does rush to judgment about its experiences. It quickly gravitates to either good or bad. But many of our experiences aren't really particularly bad or good. They're just experiences. With meditation, we begin to see our experiences through a more neutral lens. Everything that is happening right now is simply happening right now. It just is. We develop the kind of neutrality we have when we think of fruit or trees. We don't automatically judge an apple as good and an orange as bad. Nor do we usually walk in the woods wishing the pine trees were actually fir trees.

However, neutrality doesn't mean indifference. Feeling neutral is actually very freeing. When we see thoughts and remain neutral we aren't caught in *I like it* or *I don't like it*. Instead, we become curious and observant. We notice when and how our minds can get snagged. As neutrality deepens, we don't feel the need to have thoughts disappear. We can let them be, and we aren't so bothered by them. And if we aren't bothered by them then their shenanigans no longer hold us captive. As neutrality increases, the witness in us strengthens. As the witness strengthens we gain some freedom from the mind's reactions. The true witness is inherently neutral. The more we settle into the witness role, the more we don't react. The more we recognize neutrality emerging from our meditations, the more we notice neutrality spilling into our *regular* life.

Broken Dish

I remember standing in my kitchen one afternoon, holding a blue ceramic bowl full of cool, white yogurt and plump, deep red strawberries. I could taste the fruit just by looking at it. But my fingers were a little greasy from my hand lotion, and the bowl slipped. Down went my afternoon delight. The pile of smashed clay blended with yogurt and bruised fruit lay sadly at my feet. I just looked at it. I noticed how the clay and food intermingled on the linoleum. Then I waited for my body to tense up. But nothing happened. I didn't move and I didn't feel much of anything. How amazing. In the past, I would have tightened up and screeched in frustration. But I just stood there, and a profound sense of stillness took over. Now as I write this, a little voice says, *not that earth shattering*. But I know it was. The depth of my non-reaction was profound. The way I felt when I looked at the mess on the floor was reminiscent of a deep meditation. The resonance was the same. Talk about neutrality. I was becoming free of the trappings of my mind.

But neutrality over a broken bowl on the floor pointed to a much bigger issue. It reminded me of the importance of maintaining a sense of peace and calm for the benefit of those around me. By tensing up when things went wrong I had unknowingly been frightening my daughter. From my current place of calm, I now see that my strong reactions and my screeches of frustration scared her. I see this now when something goes wrong or an item goes missing or we are late for an appointment. My daughter will look at me sideways to see my reaction, to see if I am tensing up, or about to freak out. But I am not. I truly am not. I am happy to report that losses or mishaps really don't throw me off anymore. It is amazing but they just don't – good for me and great for my daughter. So if there is one good reason for us to take up meditation, it may be so we don't scare our children. But whatever your reason, trust me, if you show up regularly in your boat and sit and watch your breath, something *will* change. My ability to show up regularly helped me more than I could have known. My trust in the process of just sitting watching my breath allowed for a permanent transformation at my core. I thought, *Hey, it's really true. The unexpected does start happening.*

While we aren't always sure what to expect from a regular meditation practice, some sort of blind faith will keep us going. When we stay with the process, our world actually starts changing. Expect nothing from the process and revel in what happens. You will start to see changes in the way you perceive your entire world, once you recognize that watching has a depth of acceptance that is new and refreshing. You will learn to be grounded in exactly where you are.

With this visualization, take yourself out under the stars, either literally or figuratively, and have a look.

Night Sky

With the ground warm and firm beneath you
And the sky deep and radiant above you
You lie out under the stars
In the stillness of the night
You lie out under the stars

As a witness to the night's bounty
Darkness and light
In equal measure
You lie here in order to see
Simple seeing
You lie here in order to breathe
Simple breathing

In front of your eyes
Light and movement
In front of your eyes
The stillness of night
Watching the light
And breathing in
Watching the dark
And breathing out

The ground beneath you
A gentle reminder

To breathe and notice
That you are face to face
With the night sky
You see stars and the space around stars
You see thoughts and the space around thoughts
Watching the nothing
And breathing in
Watching the everything
And breathing out

Lights and shapes
Ideas and feelings
All continue in each other
Breathing and watching
The observer and the observed
Lights and movement
So bright and sure
And the stillness of the air
So spacious and vast

Streams of light
Cast cross the darkness
And you and night sky
Are linked by the breath
You and night sky
Are out here together
In kinship and ease

You are out here together
In darkness and light
You and night sky
You are here together
In equal measure

Watching the luminous sky and the trails of light and thought gives us an appreciation of the structure and purpose of our minds. We the observers come to understand the mind's need for purpose and busyness.

Welcoming

With these busy minds comes an array of activity and drive. Our thought patterns have a thick, dense quality, a little like congested traffic. Ideas and beliefs run to and fro, up and down, and in and out, narrowly escaping collision. When a collision does occur, we are in for an instant headache. Collision or not, we want to escape this crazy traffic scene by pushing it away. Even after years of meditating, I will now and then slip back into the habit of trying to make the thoughts I don't like go away. Then I remember not to push them away but to do something counter-intuitive. I welcome them and make them bigger. I let thoughts be huge! No repression, no feeling as though the mind should go away. Also, the bigger the thoughts are, the more easily I can see them. I can witness the roaring, the spinning and the cries for attention. I allow this display. I give the thoughts what they want. *Yes, you are big and important, and I grant you all the space and size that you need.* This allowance is very freeing. There is no repression, no containing and no holding.

By allowing thoughts to be big, we are actually eliminating any notion that we could actually push them away. They are just too big to push away. We can give way to their enormity and thus in a kind of sweet resignation we can rest in our smallness. We rest in that fact that we are almost invisible in comparison. And right here, in this virtual invisibility, lies the magic. If we allow for the suggestion that we can become invisible, and we humbly give way to the power of our thoughts to do this, then we become free. We are free of the sticky form of huge mind patterns and we are free to enter the world of non-form. And in this freedom, we become immense. Clever trick. When we are immense, we are not really a part of the busy-mind stuff. We can simply watch the mind's activities without suppressing them. In our immensity, we are not bound by size or structure, because invisibility has no form. It is as though we evaporated into a place of stillness – as though our molecules got warm enough to turn into vapor and we lifted off into another form. We were the last bubble of the existing form, and then we evaporated into another form. No thinking, just gone. Not trying just gone. But this isn't scary *gone*. This is fun *gone*, freeing *gone*.

And as we move into a state of non-form, we can watch important thoughts balloon up and show their mighty form. We just stay in our own type of immensity and keep coming back to our breath. If we slip back into busy-mind patterns, that's okay. We always have the breath. Even if the breath is the tiniest of threads weaving itself through all this crazy mind stuff, we remember the breath. The breath is our loyal companion and is dedicated to our survival. It is also very kind and generous. In fact, our whole body is very kind to us. It repairs itself every moment. When we wake up each morning we have a chance to start again – to eat better, to exercise more, and to breathe more deeply. Our body and breath kindly allow us a *do over* for as long as we are alive. Now we need to extend this infinite amount of kindness to ourselves.

Kindness

We need mountains of patience and gentleness as we bring our focus back and back again to the breath. The Sanskrit word *maitri* describes this limitless compassion and loving kindness towards ourselves and others. And we certainly need a lot of *maitri* when we see our mind wander off for the hundredth time. There is great relief in kindly accepting that our journey is full of repetitive and tenacious elements, and that it is okay to keep bringing the mind back, again and again. *Maitri* will help with this process. When your mind goes wandering off, with gentleness and a soft touch you bring it back, again and again.

Loving kindness and compassion can be seen even in the smallest gestures. I remember one summer visiting my friend Gail who had just taken in a foster dog who was a bit of a lost soul. Gail was going to be looking after the dog for a few weeks so she had to set down some ground rules. The first rule was not to eat out of the cat's bowl. This sweet dog just didn't get why he couldn't walk over to the cat's corner and eat the *delicious* food. As he made each hopeful attempt, Gail would gently guide him around to the other side of the kitchen counter to the location of *his* bowl. She led him back, over and over again. Then when she wasn't looking, he would drop his head down low, so as not to be noticed, and creep back to the cat's bowl. I was mesmerized by the dance I was seeing. Gail with a sweep of her arm, and a soft touch on his fur, would gently turn the dog towards his own bowl. The arc of her arm with the turn of his body was their dance. This went on for half an hour, no resistance, and no struggle. What incredible patience and loving kindness she showed for this sentient being. That kind of *maitri* was beautiful to watch. Now we learn to extend the same *maitri* to ourselves. With gentleness, we bring our focus back to the breath over and over again, as we continue trying to *get it right*.

Tapping

In order to bring the mind back to the breath and avoid excessive derailment, we can employ a physical reminder – tapping on the body. The tapping tells your mind that it has a job to do other than wander off every few seconds. Tapping also helps you place the breath in the body. I like to start with a gentle tap just below the ribs. I tap at random intervals maybe every 5 seconds, then maybe every 8 seconds. I don't always know the exact time of the intervals but I estimate (no strict rules). Starting with the rib area helps ground the breath deeply into my chest. As I tap, I keep bringing my breath and attention to the point of contact. After tapping for a few seconds, I let my hand rest, and then I just notice the sensation leftover from the tapping. Noticing the post tapping feeling in my chest keeps me focused.

Now here is where I run into a bit of a problem. I am trying to watch the breath and watch the thoughts as they dance by, without engaging the mind too much. But the tapping *does* engage the mind. I *do* have to use some brain cells in order to remind myself to tap. So I decide to only use those few brain cells that like to repeat mindless tasks. This way the mind engagement is minimal and constructive. After the tapping I can then just settle back into the sensations in my body where I was just tapping – sensations on the surface of my skin such as heat or tingling. Then I tap again in the same spot but this time I take my breath with me. Meaning that I imagine that the sole entry and exit of the in and out breath happen right in this spot where I have been tapping. The breath expands and contracts right there in my chest; right inside the heat and tingling. I keep strengthening the feeling of my chest being breathed. The repetition becomes very interesting and even fun after awhile – trust me.

The tapping exercise helps us to become mindful of where our body is and where our breath is. It brings awareness into physical sensation and out of the head, and gives the wandering mind something to hold on to. The exercise can be likened to someone tapping you on the shoulder and saying, *Hey, we're over here. We're focusing on this right now.*

The chest tapping and breath expansion was working well for me, but I wanted to go even further down into the body and as far away from my busy mind as I could. So, I went to the feet. Just as I had done with the chest tapping, I would tap on the bottom of each foot, then wait a few seconds and then notice the sensation left over from the tapping. I repeated the tapping and noticing. I looked for changes in sensation after each tap. Was the sensation strong, weak, warm, vibrating? Whatever the sensation, I used the power of my mind to increase and hold that sensation. I let my breath direct the sensations down through my feet and into the floor. I kept remembering that my mind could do anything that I tasked it with. Using the bottom of the feet helped anchor me into the ground, and helped curtail the endless thought trails.

Drinking Water

An everyday activity such as sipping on a glass of water can also teach us about the endless possibilities of meditation experiences. Sipping on water takes us inside our body, and provides us with the felt sense of cool liquid entering our body. It is amazing how many times we drink water without knowing or noticing where and how the water moves through the body. So I started noticing. With each sip of water, I would follow the cool sensation of the water as it slid over the back of my tongue, down my throat, into my esophagus and down to my stomach. I would follow the water like a thread winding its way deep into my body. The coolness and the depth were the key sensations that I focused on. When my mind popped in and said, *I am just drinking water. What's the big deal?* I would thank it for its input and go back to feeling the sensation of water moving through my body. The cool thread of water had my full attention. The sensation of the water was the physical reminder of where I wanted my mind to go. I wanted my busy mind to take its attention on a ride along the thread of cool water. After awhile, my mind finally flipped over into only sensing, and flipped out of cognitive awareness of the process of drinking.

This flip out of busy-mind is key. As soon as we flip out of the cognitive awareness of drinking water, we are out of form and into sensation. The physical act of drinking water is part of our world of form and thought. The felt sense of the depth reached by the water represents the world of spacious awareness outside of form and thought. Our distinction between cognitive awareness and felt awareness allows us to stay anchored in an experience that until now has been outside our daily radar.

Other Anchors

We can use other physical anchors to feel the depth of non-form and non-thought. A slight weight on our chest can take us down into a felt sense of breath. When lying on my couch, I place a small pillow on my chest, and begin to watch my breath. Having a light weight on my chest anchors my attention to that part of my body and brings my attention very clearly to my breath. The up and down movement of the pillow matches the rising and falling of my inhalation and exhalation. I can then sink deeply into the nuances of breath. And just as I did when sipping water, I watch for the moment when I stop thinking about the pillow on my chest, and flip into the awareness of only air and movement. The breathing sensations don't need to be articulated in my mind. They are felt in my body. Every time we notice the flip – the moment when we move out of form and into sensation – we are once again finding that air space that lives in and around our busy minds. By practicing the flip, with water or weight, we are reinforcing our knowing of this new place. The more we intentionally make this flip, by practicing, the more we will unintentionally move into this new awareness at any given moment.

After a little time with the tapping, the drinking water, or the weight on the chest exercises, you will start to get a sense of how your mind works, or rather doesn't work. You will begin to develop your own images and metaphors that take you beyond the mind's questions and analyzing. Go with these images. The body/breath team is coming up with its own creative way into the new air space. Let your imagination have its way. Being fluid with your techniques keeps you open-minded, flexible and curious.

Use this next visualization to create images for yourself that capture you; images that encourage you to fall back, with your arms held out, suspended by your own imagination.

Floating On Your Back

With the grace of the ocean beneath you
You can lie right here on your back
Kept afloat
By the rhythm of your breath
Kept afloat by the weight of the water
Floating on your back
Arms spread wider than you can see

Giving in
To everything that moves around you
To everything that stirs within you
At the mercy of your whole life
You surrender
Floating with the rhythm of the water
Your skin and bones suspended
By small movements
And small waves
By slow breathing
And deep rhythm
Floating on your back
You are weightless... like a leaf

Resting on the surface of the ocean
Your body floating
In the place
Where air and water meet
Below you
Water rippling and shuddering
With the texture of form and mind
Above you
A bare and generous sky
Open and empty and wide

Floating with the rhythm of water
You are the space between air and water
You are the gap
Between thought and no thought
You watch what is above you
You feel what is below you
You are the connection
Between full and empty
Your breath steadies you
With a certainty
That reaches out beyond thought

And you know that lying here on your back
Eyes on the vastness
Is all you know
Is all you need
Breathing in
Sky above you
Breathing out
Water below you
Breathing in
Wind around you
Breathing out
Grace within you

With breath that is slow and sure
You can spread your arms out wide
And be a willing body to
The waves
The water
The movement
You let everything happen to you
You're all in

After floating and breathing on the surface of the water, you understand that you are right where you need to be. And watching and feeling, in this moment, is all right.

Pure Seeing

As we rest in the simplicity of watching, we are able to suspend thought and trust in the simpler process of just observing. Recognition of a new state of openness or emptiness begins to occur. And then our mind comes in with a whole list of objections: *What is openness? What is emptiness? Does emptiness mean I have nothing?* Don't worry about the questions, or the answers. Just suspend judgment and keep watching.

Watching is about really seeing what is right in front of us without filters or judgments. We can start to see events without the labels of high or low, worthy or unworthy, in or out, or good or bad. We have no filters, just pure seeing, the way young children see the world. A child has not had time to develop thick filters. When we hear children's perceptions of life, their pure seeing can trigger a new awareness in us. This is how some young children see love:

> When you love somebody, your eyelashes go up and down and little
>   stars come out of you. Karen, age 7
> Love is what's in the room with you at Christmas if you stop
>   opening presents and listen. Bobby, age 7
> When someone loves you, the way they say your name is different.
>   You just know that your name is safe in their mouth.[3] Billy, age 4

Listening to children can help us see differently. After some years of life's twists and turns, we don't always see what is right in front of us. We have learned to drop our heads and push ahead, without looking up. This blind pushing does not serve us well. So now we decide to look up and watch, and we take in what is around us.

Looking at Pain

Just as we watch thoughts going by, we can begin to watch physical pain as an interesting phenomenon. However, pain is only interesting if it is not overwhelming. If your pain level is tolerable enough that you are somewhat functional, then you will be able to take a look at your discomfort/pain from a slightly different angle. After hearing Bud's story at the gas station, I started thinking about pain and meditation. Since meditation is about calming the mind, then meditation, once taken into the body, could also be about calming the phenomena that occur in the body, like physical pain. Bud described the chronic pain in his chest after three surgeries. I think it would be fair to say that Bud was somewhat functional in his life, since he was able to work, but he still needed to deal with the chronic pain. Bud's first few steps into the world of meditation would help him to see the possibilities. By observing his thoughts and then writing them down, Bud would learn about watching and witnessing. As he strengthened his ability to witness he would begin to feel a little distance from his pain.

With meditation, dealing with aches and pains is possible and oddly intriguing. We start with those aches and pains that are somewhat tolerable and we work with the more challenging pain later. I would start by taking my attention to a somewhat tolerable ache or pain such as a slight headache, a tingling pain in my knee, or a tight, achy shoulder. Once I was relatively comfortable I would close my eyes and focus on the painful area, bringing the pain into clear view as though I was looking at it under a microscope. I wanted to observe every little nuance of the pain. I thought of advertising graphics that promote pain products, in which pain was depicted in the form of an animated throbbing image. I would borrow that throbbing image and exaggerate it in my mind. I would see the expansion and contraction of the bones in the head, or the throbbing and pulsing of the blood in my knee. I welcomed a strong and dramatic image. Then I would slow down my breath, by making my exhalation longer, and direct the breath to the painful area. A slow breath was key to keeping my focus. As I inhaled, I would imagine the painful area expanding. As I exhaled, I would imagine the painful area contracting. With the in and out breaths, I was getting movement, and ultimately air space, into the area in question. I was seeing how pain behaves. I was focusing on the throbbing and pulsing phenomenon as a curious observer. I would watch pain this way for awhile to see how it behaved under observation.

So Now What?

At the beginning of this chapter, we started off with the simple goal of just watching the breath, and we didn't plan for great moments. We anchored ourselves in the simple act of watching. We observed thoughts and came back to the breath, over and over again with lightness, kindness and generosity. We came back to seeing what was in front of us. The watching tool is always available to us, and after a while our ability to *really* see becomes second nature. Then when we aren't looking, some great moments do arise among the ruins of busy-mind. Clarity, understanding and a welcome quiet all start to occur – just by watching.

And even though we started out intending not to meditate, guess what? We actually did meditate. As soon as we became the observer and we were able to establish even the smallest amount of breathing space between ourselves and our busy minds, we were meditating. This new breathing space grounds us and allows us to see and know the reality of our actual selves – our core selves. Not the selves that are run ragged by busy-mind.

When I first heard spiritual teachers talk about our *actual self* or our *true self*, I really had no idea what they were talking about. Wasn't I really me already? Then I got it. The chaotic thought patterns of my mind were not actually me. The thought patterns were just ideas and projections floating around in my head. I understood that my busy mind was like the TV show I had forgotten to turn off. On the TV, a scene would be playing out about somebody, somewhere, doing something dramatic, and I would forget where I was. My consciousness and my body together thought that the TV show was real and the show's events were the only reality there was, for that moment. Fortunately, something would jolt me out of this unconscious state and I would have to ask myself, *Where am I? Where is the actual me who is **not** part of this TV show? What am **I** really doing right now, or next week or for the next decade?* Then I would know that I needed to turn off the TV, grab my knees, rub my shoulders and tug at my hair. I needed to find the core me, separate from a reality that wasn't a reality. The TV show was like my thoughts – busy, dramatic and distracting. The TV show and my busy mind tugged at me and took me away from the core element that was just about simple breathing and simple seeing. My core self needed to emerge and take over.

Often my simple, breathing core self would come up against some interesting phenomena. During one meditation the theme was all about time. I had decided to sit for an hour. Within this hour I wanted to explore the difference between thinking and the sweet place just outside of thinking that doesn't seem to know time. Actually I didn't really want to explore the difference. I really wanted to just stay in the sweet non-thinking place for the whole hour accepting that the busy thinking place was close by. But wanting and reality weren't jiving. Then I remembered – watch and accept. Got it.

So I proceeded with the meditation in the usual way – watching the breath, slipping into this place of breath that didn't know time, then falling back into the place of thinking and time awareness, then suddenly falling back into non-thinking and no time awareness, and so on. There were moments in which I was wonderfully lost in the place that was expansive and simply didn't recognize that there were exactly 42 minutes to go before

I would get back to thinking. The whole concept of minutes and seconds was foreign to this place. This place didn't know time.

Then there were those moments in which I was instantly pulled back into the thinking, time-oriented place 36 minutes to go. This thinking place was very well acquainted with time. It loved schedules and structure, and identified with starting points and ending points. It pulled me back with a power that was almost uncomfortable. Important messages about a chore that needed doing, or a worry that needed attending to, or some food that needed eating, defined its purpose.

As I moved back and forth, or rather was pulled back and forth, I recognized a strange longing to be in *both* places. Yes I wanted to stay in the sweet expanse that knew no time and felt like freedom and relief. But yes, I sort of wanted to get back to the familiarity of good old thinking and doing. I felt the longing for both and the ensuing pull in my body. So, what to do? I decided just to state the facts, to see what was true. The facts as I saw them were that the thinking mind was familiar and oddly powerful, and the non-thinking place knew no time. That is all I could surmise at the time. With the facts on the table, I felt less longing and grasping, in both directions.

So I went on with the meditation and when I slipped into the sweet, not-so-much thinking expanse, I just kept stating the fact *this place doesn't know time, this place doesn't know time*. If I kept saying, *this place doesn't know time*, then I felt free of the wanting to stay there because I was just stating a fact. My whole body and mind relaxed into that fact. I could stop being caught in trying to get to one or the other. Watching what was happening and seeing what was true freed me up. I carried on with this new approach. After awhile, I glanced over at the clock – one minute to go.

With a little distance between our simple breathing self and our complex thinking self, we can see things more clearly. We are starting to generate a change from inside out. And the ability to breathe a little easier is a welcome relief. Now it's time to step back.

Chapter Three

Stepping Back

When we live with the same mind for many years, our way of being is predictable and familiar. Our mind's reactions have become hard-coded habits, which help us sleep the years away, without even knowing we are sleeping. Our mind is like our old town or neighborhood that defines our life and our under-standing of how the world works.

In our town, we know the streets, the ditches, the hills and the paths. We see the same road signs staring back at us day after day, year after year. In our minds, we know the thoughts, the worries, the fears and the hopes. We hear the same thoughts playing over and over again, day after day, year after year. In town, we get home by taking the same old turn at the second street on the left, followed by the first right after the lights. In our minds, we get comfortable with the familiar and predictable thoughts. As we head through town, we are reminded of our habitual thought patterns taking their known twists and turns. All this familiarity provides us with a daily sedative with which we can easily lose a tangible sense of the present moment.

It's time to take a walk. We need to hike up the hill at the edge of town and have a look. We need to step back from the whole scene. With just a small amount of distance, our perceptions change. The meandering streets and wandering thoughts will take on a new look when we stand at the edge of town looking back. Our step back will involve conviction and breath. We will learn to move with the breath into the air space that holds more answers than questions, and calls out to us with a distinct voice. When we step back, we slide in behind thoughts when they aren't looking. We enter our found air space and breathe a sigh of relief.

The air space we enter is really the part of our core selves that is vast and limitless, and we step back into it by learning to fall away rather than push away. In *Stillness Speaks*, Eckart Tolle writes of the quiet awareness that exists when we have "*stepped out of thousands of years of collective human conditioning.*"[4] When we step back we unhinge from the unconscious patterns that run our lives. When we step back, we become aware of a profound and inherent quiet that *is* us.

So how do we get there? We start by tapping into that little bit of blind faith we may have tucked away somewhere. Now is the time to resurrect our conviction that, as daunting as this journey sounds, we can find our way to meditation in a new way. We remember that when our rational brain hears about finding some lost air space, it doesn't have any experience to support the concept. But then we remember that we are going on a journey that takes us outside the workings of the rational mind. The journey isn't long in distance but it is huge in dimension.

How Far Back?

How far away is this lost air space? It's closer than we think. Let's go to early morning when we are sleeping in our beds, head on the pillow and covers wrapped around us. We could be dreaming of anything from the mundane to the bizarre, and all things in between. At some point we 'wake up'. What just happened? How far did we just go? Our bodies are basically in the same position – no traveling there. Our room looks pretty much the same. Other than the clock saying something different, everything on the outside looks pretty much the same yet everything on the inside changed completely in a split second. We just moved from a dream state to waking consciousness.

We are no longer part of those dream images and situations. We are no longer identified with those events. We are awake in our beds rubbing our eyes, and running through the memories from the night before. Or we are awake in our room not really sure what went on in the last few hours. Either way, everything changed in an instant. As though we turned our heads slightly in one direction or the other, and we were somewhere else – two degrees to the left or two breaths to the right, and we were awake. The transition was so slight, yet our world is now so different. We are back in our thinking minds, back to *normal*. We have our thoughts, plans, memories and hopes. We carry on with the business of our lives, our journey from birth to death and everything in between. But remember, we only moved about two imperceptible degrees in order to enter waking consciousness.

Now, what if we move another two degrees away from waking consciousness? What if we take the same short journey we took from sleep to awake, to find another shift in consciousness? This short journey happens when we step back into that kind of air space that contains an exquisite emptiness called the present moment.

The same distance that we travel from dreaming to wakefulness is the same distance that we travel from awake to empty. We can step back two degrees and land in a kind of emptiness that feels like nothing and everything at the same time. But sometimes the word *emptiness* can be scary. However, emptiness does not mean non-existence. It just means that we are empty of distractions and preoccupations, and we are therefore full of a spacious stillness. Emptiness provides a place for us to experience the newly-found air space.

We often think that meditators must spend many years in practice in order to decrease the chaos of the mind, and to travel to this beautiful empty place that is not ruled by time or form – a place that just is. However, even though years of practice do strengthen your ability to move into this place, beginners can also find it in an instant. Because the transition is only two degrees or two breaths away, it is relatively easy to locate. Part of the location process includes our ability to feel, name and imagine a place that is empty of chaos, and full of quiet. Many teachers, awakened beings, mystics, and regular folk have felt and beautifully described this emptiness and quiet. Yet, each one of us has to put our own words to this experience. Each one of us needs to trust that we can get there, and that our experience will be different from anyone else's.

Time to Step

To feel the first step back, we start by inhaling and doing nothing. Then we exhale and take an imaginary and barely perceptible step back. In so doing, we create a very subtle and slight separation between us the watcher and us the busy-mind. We shift from being immersed in thoughts to simply seeing them, just there in front of us. Imagine a thin veil that you could hold in your fingertips. One side of the veil holds a place for thinking and worrying, while the other side holds open space that is so free of thought that you could just fall back in, and sigh. Both sides exist right up against the veil. They are each only two degrees from each other. Imagine stepping back through the veil that has been holding you inside the mind, and suddenly feeling the air space that lies outside your busy mind. This cool, sweet air is a welcome surprise. Who knew? How great that there is this place of expansive and generous air that invites us in to breathe and rest.

This air space sits right in this present moment. It is not bound by the trails of thoughts that take us into the past, where we can ruminate over what did happen, nor is it tied to the thoughts that hypothesize about what might happen. This air space exists in the *only* moment that we truly have – this moment. It provides plenty of room for viewing the reality of what is happening just now.

Noticing

Once you get your first sensation of this spacious resting place, you may want to hold on for dear life because it feels so good. But holding on or grasping for the stillness just creates the same old tension and resistance we talked about earlier. We grasp for what we want by trying to push away our thoughts so we can get back to this quiet place. Learning and re-learning not to create tension is tricky and subtle. Again, we go back to noticing the tension we create by grasping for stillness and wanting the meditation to work. But trying to make it *work* isn't going to get us anywhere. So we imagine the feeling of not trying to make it work. Then we look at the sense of relief of not trying to make it work because we just gave up on the whole idea of trying. We notice trying and working at it, and then we notice not trying and not working at it. We practice alternating between the two. As we alternate, we learn to feel the subtle difference between tension and ease, between thought and no thought. We start by saying to ourselves, *I am aware that I have many thoughts. I am aware that my mind is racing. I am aware that I am breathing and I am aware that I can step back.*

During this process, all kinds of thoughts will arise. Sorrow, joy, frustration, elation, anger and regret are just a few, and they all play their part. There will be questioning, analyzing and criticizing thoughts. When we were watching we learned to sit and just be with the emotions and thoughts that arose. We learned to differentiate between busy-mind patterns and our core selves, without dissociating from thoughts. When we differentiate in meditation, we recognize that both parts exist simultaneously. Thoughts hang out over there and our essential awareness or core self hangs out over here. We are beside thoughts; we live with them but we recognize that they are different from our core selves. And at our core we are these immense, glorious, breathing beings who live with thoughts but are differentiated from thoughts. We don't try to suppress or annihilate thoughts, we simply move in and around them.

But when we dissociate in meditation, we push thoughts away to the point where they appear not to exist. We either suppress or annihilate thoughts, which requires a good deal of pushing and tension. And if thoughts are suppressed through pushing and tension we aren't free. We are ironically quite attached to what we have repressed because it can have a hold on us.

So we build our awareness of differentiation versus dissociation. And we soon learn that there is a very fine line between the two. At any given moment you could be merrily going along in your differentiation meditation and then realize you have just been putting in a good effort wishing that a particular thought simply didn't exist. I notice this phenomenon in many of my meditations. In fact, on an inhalation I could be accepting, watching and stepping back, all very cooperatively. Then on the very next exhalation, I am pushing, tugging and earnestly trying to repress an annoying thought. So I say to myself, *Oh well*, and I keep going.

With compassion and a little humor, we watch the antics of the mind. We begin to recognize the difference between the mind's endless activities and tricks, and the still self that can be with things just as they are. When thoughts seem particularly unruly, you can simply look right at them and say, *I am aware that you exist and that you have important things to say and feel*. Then go back to the sensation of stepping back, and the intention not to push thoughts away as you step back. Go back to feeling the subtle difference between tension and ease, between thought and no thought. Once you are very familiar with tension versus non-tension, you can get ready to take another step back.

Picturing It

You can create your own powerful image of stepping back. You can make this image as rich and vibrant as you like. Allow yourself to sense the stepping back, and to experience and feel what kind of place you are stepping into. As soon as you have a picture of this place, step back into it and allow yourself to feel as though you can very easily just fall into this new spaciousness.

What if you couldn't help but fall in? Believe me, your mind is powerful and capable enough to imagine all of this, with flare. You step back into a place that is not ruled by thought. Stepping back is just about finding a new location for yourself, so you are not so entangled with the mind. Remember that you aren't going very far, just far enough to feel a differentiation between thought and non-thought; just two degrees or two breaths away from where you started. And you *want* this first step to be small. If you get too far away from thoughts there is a good chance that the thoughts will get repressed or pushed away. Keep thoughts close so you can keep an eye on them. Keep just enough distance to allow for a little air space between you and them. If some thoughts leap over the air space and attach themselves to you, just step back again.

When you see or feel a particularly sticky thought you might be inclined to say, *I don't like this thought* or *maybe I should think about this right now* or *I am bored with thinking of this again and again.* Endless trials of demanding thoughts will try to get your attention. For now though, just say, *Hmm, that's interesting,* and step back again. You can allow yourself to flip back and forth between the demanding thoughts and the *that's interesting* approach, again and again. As you flip back and forth, notice the very subtle difference in sensations in your body. The demanding thoughts engage the mind with a firm grip. You can notice how that grip translates to sensation. The *that's interesting* approach can feel like an unhinging, and can show up in the body as a new sensation.

Zero in on the subtleties here, and keep your eye on body sensations. If the demanding thoughts seem to take charge, just notice their demands, and remember that most of them will be gone in a matter of hours or days. This process is repetitive yet intriguing. Knowledge of our mind's activities leads to pretty clear insights down the road. As always, remember to apply *maitri* on this road. We need to be kind to ourselves because we will be stepping back into this new spaciousness, over and over again, for quite some time.

And as fast as we discover this new air space full of rest and quiet, that's how fast we can lose track of it. The truth is that we will go in and out of recognition of this place all the time and we need to remind ourselves not to push. We will learn to step back from our busy mind with care and subtlety. But alas, we *will* tend to create tension and repress thoughts as we learn our way through this. In fact, we will probably have this tendency for the rest of our lives because our inclination to either let thoughts run rampant or repress them is well conditioned. This tendency lives in us, though we don't often see it or feel it. Even those of us who have been on this meditation journey for some time will unknowingly repress thought and have to remind ourselves to take notice, and step back again.

Side By Side

If you are worried about what happens to your busy mind when you step back into an air space of no thought, don't be. When we step back we haven't lost anything. The two worlds – thought versus no thought – live side by side; we don't have to get rid of one in order to be in the other. We *can* slip away from our overzealous thoughts without annihilating them. The worlds coexist within very close proximity. They exist as two corridors side by side. No matter how active one corridor is, with its moods, concepts and emotions, the other corridor is always the same... empty, spacious, free and quiet. Both are happening at the *same* time, so there is no pressure, no force, and no push. If you get confused during this process remember to ask yourself, *Where am I in all of this?* Getting your whereabouts helps you stay on track. If you have slipped back into the busy-mind corridor, then calmly step back again into the quiet. You locate your core self in your quiet corridor.

The notion of side by side is useful because it doesn't create pressure. There is no force needed to simply step back or step to one side. Side by side is a gentle, horizontal maneuver that lends itself to a sense of ease because nothing is being forced down. Forcing and suppressing are all too common in the world of meditation. In fact, many people meditate for years by sitting on their busy minds. Thoughts, emotions, and reactions are very neatly tucked away somewhere deep in the body. It is as if from the neck up they are all smiles and peaceful, and from the neck down, who knows what is going on. Please note that I am not entirely excluding myself from this group. Every time I meditate, I believe that some sort of suppression occurs. I am constantly on the lookout for a sense of pushing away, pushing down or simply annihilating. To combat this tendency, I keep looking for creative and interesting imagery that allows for the world of thought to coexist with the world of non-thought. The form of thoughts, ideas, and concepts can be right beside no form. Form and formless live horizontally.

Your imagination will take you very far with this side-by-side approach to meditation. The busy-mind corridor of thought and form can be right up against the quiet corridor of non-thought and non-form. Imagine how you can move freely between the two. Keep in mind that the images that you use, as you step back or step to the side, are of your own making. Be creative. Experiment and find what suits your sensibilities. As you read this next visualization, remember to pause between each stanza, and see your own corridors come into view.

Cocktail Party

There you stand in a room
Any room, anywhere
With no particular address
In no particular place
A luscious room full of life, noise, excitement

Worry, sadness and hope
All of the ingredients of your busy life
Your busy mind

Each ingredient taking its own form
Each thought and each idea securing its own voice
Saying who it is
Saying what it wants
Each voice becoming its own person

There you stand surrounded by your people
Standing in the middle
Watching
And nodding
Seeing who they are
Some are tall
Some are round
Some are angry
And some are proud
Your thoughts, your people
Expressing themselves through color
Through movement, through talk

Standing in the middle of their party
You hear how important they are
How right they are
How sad they feel
You hear all of their stories
And you love them for their efforts
And their sincerity
You admire them for their tenacity

And their endurance
They talk to you

They talk to each other
And they talk to themselves
They talk quickly and endlessly

Your people, your thoughts
You watch, you listen
And you begin to step back
Taking small steps
Quietly and unnoticed
Stepping back
Feeling your toes then your heels
On the party room floor

Placing one foot behind the other
Moving slowly
Moving gently
Not to disturb
Not to judge
Just to see, then take your leave
You keep stepping back
With ease and silence
You send them good will
As you reach for the door

A crack in the doorway
Is your quiet way out
Sliding through
You step away... into

Into a quiet
A stillness
Empty of chaos
And full of silence
Nothing you can describe in words

A vacuum of rhythmic breath sounds
Everything
And nothing
A place to be
A place to let everything just stop

With a glance back over your shoulder
At the light coming through the door
You know what is there
And you exhale
You stand in a vacuum of open breath
Still and quiet
Now you stand in a place
With no particular anything

As you stand in this unique place, you know that something new is possible. You know that you have the ability to imagine and find a place that is oddly familiar, as though you were there once in a dream. This quiet corridor will serve you well, and you can make a note-to-self about going back there as often as you can.

Understanding the concept of side by side leads us to one of the essential elements of meditation – the unlearning of our tendency to fix a problem. Instead of trying to change or get away from our busy mind, we strengthen what is *not* our busy mind. Our busy mind with its myriad of thought patterns is busy and seemingly purposeful at every moment. An inherent momentum drives our busy mind. This momentum seems to push beyond what is reasonable. We can easily get confused and think that the thinking is all there is! So we step away and let the momentum carry on, on its own. Instead of focusing on this momentum that is endlessly racing, we focus on what *isn't* racing. We focus on and strengthen the quiet, air space that sits right beside our busy mind. This change in focus is key to allowing our intention to relax. It is also key to reducing our tendency to fix the problem of a constantly thinking mind. We just leave it be. And we don't need years of training to find that core of air space that is stillness. We can find that in an instant. What we may need though is years of reminding ourselves that we can find that place in an instant.

Multitasking

A close cousin to the notion of side by side is multitasking. Whether we think we are good at multitasking or not, we are all doing it in varying degrees all of the time. On any given day, we could be sitting in our living room watching the news, waiting for a call, eating a snack, and checking our email. Then someone walks into the room and asks us to listening for a knock at the door because they are expecting a delivery. No problem. We just add listening for the knock to the list. When the knock does arrive, our focus on the front door and the impending delivery is suddenly stronger than our focus on the other four tasks. The knock is all encompassing. Soon the delivery task is complete. Okay, back to doing the four other activities.

Now, what if someone came into the room and asked us to add watching the breath to our four other activities? That could be possible. After all, we easily accepted the job of adding listening for the knock, without any hesitation. So watching the breath could just be added to our moments of multitasking. Sounds simple. We simply take a part of our multitasking awareness to the fact that air goes in and out of our bodies every few seconds. Once we are comfortable with our fifth activity, we pretend that the breathing is now like the knock at the door. It needs our full attention for a few minutes. By noticing the breath, we are taking one layer of our multitasking ability and giving it more attention. In so doing, the other four layers fade into the background and the breathing layer gets stronger. We are side by side with the other four layers, but we have made a choice to make the fifth layer, watching the breath, a priority. The breathing layer becomes the quiet corridor that we step into more and more often. And the other four layers become the corridor of busyness that exists close by. We understand corridors through our familiarity with multitasking. Soon, we are using our multitasking skills to learn to 'un-multitask' and find our way to meditation.

The notion of multitasking reminds us that we can have two or more activities happening at the same time. At any point in time, we can decide to focus on one activity over the other. We are always making small choices every day as to what to focus on. Focusing on the breath layer can be the activity upon which we choose to put our attention. Meditation is really just a choice.

Shadowing

Another close cousin to the notion of side by side is *shadowing* which takes our two corridors, coexisting in very close proximity, and has them move together. This is a subtle yet pivotal concept. Essentially, one corridor will shadow the other corridor, and the two will move as one. Think of a piano player whose left hand is executing a different chord or finger pattern than the right hand but the two hands are part of the same song. Your busy-mind corridor with its moods, concepts and emotions, and your still corridor with its emptiness and quiet will move together.

For example, you could be sitting on your couch, having *shown up* for your meditation, and you have found, for a few seconds, that quiet place of non-thought and non-form. Then suddenly you pop back into busy-mind and you realize that you must have a glass of water from the kitchen. Okay, no problem. As you stand up, bring that feeling of non-thought and non-form with you. Imagine that the busy-mind-you is being shadowed by the empty-quiet-you. As you walk down the hall, you can feel presence and stillness attached to you. They are tracking your every move, shadowing you, and it feels good. You don't have to lose that still, quiet, present feeling in order to get a glass of water. Nor do you have to lose that feeling when you walk outside or run an errand or do a task. Your deep core of stillness is your essential nature and it is always with you. It shadows you like a friendly companion. Just as we can't really lose our shadow, so too, we never really step out of the state of presence. We may just lose awareness of this state.

When we understand shadowing we are able to see meditation as a real part of our lives. With meditation we become aware that there is an essence of our being that is always anchored in presence. Presence is real and it is happening all the time just as our breath is happening all the time. In a way presence *is* the breath. Shadowing helps us to recognize the continuum from meditation to daily life. And this isn't the dark side of the meaning of shadow, this is the companion side. The shadowing of presence is a comrade who walks with you, and reminds you about a core state of stillness.

This shadowing concept is, however, a little tricky. Play around with it. Imagine a way to feel as though you are still meditating when you aren't officially meditating. Find a way for the two corridors, form and non-form, to move in sync, as though each corridor was taking the other by the hand throughout the day. Once you have a sense of this shadowing feeling, you will begin to notice that you *can* be in chaos while still in quiet. You can be in a room full of activity and distractions and still feel your shadowing friend with you, beside you and around you. And as many times as you can feel a sense of shadowing, and you realize that it *is* possible, you can easily forget about *shadowing* altogether. You forget that you can be accompanied by stillness. Forgetting and then remembering are part of the process.

Amnesia

Everyday, we unconsciously get caught up in our customary activities. We react, we feel tense, we rejoice and we stew – just the regular stuff. At some point, we realize that we forgot what we learned in meditation. *What was that feeling or insight I had during my meditation? I have no idea. But I remember it seemed rather profound.* The forgetting takes us back to our hometown/busy-mind where we feel as though nothing has changed. The meditation experience that was different, exciting and freeing has slipped our mind. We need to trigger our memory a little. So here we go again. We climb back up the hill at the edge of town and step back again.

When you find your way back to the sweet place of air and nothingness, you will probably say, *Oh yeah, this is what that was! No really, I honestly completely forgot about this place and what it can feel like.* So you keep finding your way back. If your feet have some sort of amnesia about how to get back there, you can imagine a thin thread of awareness that leads you back to the air space. As you follow this thread you will come to know it by its other name – the breath. And again, you recall that your breath is always with you and it has a tremendous memory. It never fails to come back again and again, so you accept its usefulness and single-minded focus.

To remember about meditation and the breath during your day, you can pick any word that brings back the memory of that air space where breath and quiet live. The first word that comes to mind – and that fairly describes the feeling – is the one to pick. I have used words such as cavernous, breathy, airy, or empty. Your word could be different each day or could be the word that stays with you for a while or forever.

The process of remembering has another twist. You have finally recalled that different and perhaps profound place you had found yourself in when you meditated and you are ready to head back there. Okay off you go. *Wait! How do I meditate again?* That's right, we forget *how* to meditate as well. We just know that we have an interesting place to go. So, we go back to the basics. We head back to the beginning – find the breath, watch the breath, and follow the breath. The watching and the breathing, again and again, may sound annoyingly repetitive but really it is surprisingly effective. Going back to the beginning just mean you are reinforcing the 'work' you have done. Breath, start again, breath and then start again. Your mind may object because it thinks that heading back to the starting point means you are going backwards. But you are not. You are resting back into a foundation of inherent stillness. You watch and breathe over and over again as you relax into in this foundation. You crawl back in and find that thread of breath that has buried itself in the depths of amnesia.

Plenty of Room

When we step back from our chaotic and busy thought storm, we can see our busy mind as though it were laid out before us. But within a few seconds of stepping back we are *thinking* about what is laid out before us rather than just seeing it. Then we are thinking about thinking. These mental processes are familiar and habitual and can be very restrictive. Busy thoughts circle in on each other creating a tangle in which free airspace is limited. Yet, because this tight tangle of thoughts is familiar, we might not always feel so sure about leaving. We are used to close quarters. Sometimes, wide-open spaces are uncomfortable. So as we step back we may want to grab hold of something. Don't worry, no need to hold on. You won't fall in the usual sense of the word. You expand into a different kind of being. You will exist beyond the boundaries of your mind, a mind that has been using traditional concepts to define space versus no space. You will soon come to love this unencumbered place that is free of tangled and knotted thoughts.

And don't worry about bumping into anything either. There is limitless space behind us into which we can keep stepping back. No need to look over our shoulders. There is no wall to hit. In fact, the more we step back, the bigger this air space becomes.

Reversing Our Thinking

Considering that our minds can behave like unruly children, I think it is fair to apply some basic reverse psychology, when the mind isn't looking. As simple as it sounds, if we change how we perceive our thoughts or our distractions, we change our experience. When you start to feel as though your thoughts are so invasive and tenacious that stepping back from them seems impossible, then change the scenario. You can *pretend* that you *can't* hold on to your thoughts, at all. See them slipping through your fingers like water in the hand. You *can't* keep them near you or let them bother you, even if you wanted to. Surprisingly, this actually works. Remember, childlike mind calls for the simplest of approaches.

This reverse thinking is helpful in many situations. Let's say you are having a conflict at work, or your children are bringing out your inner *shenpa*. Now what? You are pretty sure that you can't easily step back at this moment because emotions such as anxiety, rage or fear are very clingy. So you reverse the way you see it. Instead of allowing strong emotions to overtake you, you figure out a way to put them to work. This idea may seem impossible but bear with me and bring out the actor in you. You know that feeling of always wanting to be on stage and always knowing you would be good at it? Well, here is your chance. We are going to act our way through this. Act as though you *want* the strong reactive emotions to stay close to you, so you can take a closer look at them. Act as though you *don't* want to repress them or run away from them, or have them disappear. As you keep bringing them close to you, pretend that they just fall away from you, slipping through your fingers. You can't hold on to them. Now notice how your mind comes in and says *This is silly*. Or *This won't work*. Acknowledge these comments and keep going. Pull the strong emotions to you again and again, and then watch them slip away. You start to realize that this mind stuff is all just a game. Your thoughts don't really *have* you.

Let this next visualization strengthen your inner actor. Turn

your thoughts into water and let that water just run through your
fingers. Sit back, hold your hands out and let the water run.

Water in the Hand

Sitting at the water's edge
Soft sand beneath you
Warm water
Moving and swaying
Around you

Sitting quietly
Feeling your breath
Still and quiet
Feeling your breath
Soft and easy
Rising and falling
As you inhale, your breath rises
As you exhale, your breath falls away

Over and over again
Rising and falling away
Then sliding down and down
Into the water
Beneath you
Sliding in, becoming water
Now as you inhale
Your thoughts begin to rise
And as you exhale
Your thoughts begin to fall away

Over and over again
Rising and then falling away
Then sliding down and down again

Into the water... Beneath you
Sliding in... becoming water
Breath becoming water
Thoughts becoming water
Sliding in
Falling away
Into water, into vastness
Thoughts falling
Becoming water
They leave behind
Exquisite space
A delicious emptiness
So light, so precious and so still

In this stillness, you reach for your thoughts
You reach into the water
Picking them up in handfuls
To see if they are still yours
But they fall back through your fingers
Again, you draw your thoughts to you
In handfuls of water
But they are wet, slippery, and elusive
As they fall away
You can't hold on to them
They are water in the hand
You draw them to you again
And they are gone again
Sliding through your fingers
Falling away
Becoming water

You are free again
Free to sit in the stillness
At the water's edge

With water running through our fingers, we realize that we are not bound by our busy mind, and that we can feel some sort of spaciousness in and around thought.

The Pause

Sometimes during a conversation or just when we are having our own little thinking party, we have trouble remembering a word or a name. The harder we try to bring this word or name to mind, the further it seems to go from us. If we take a moment, and stop trying to recall it, the word or name will pop into our heads. It rises out of our stillness, our time away. Stepping back equates to this time away; this pause in which we experience a respite from thinking. The pause is the space between thoughts in which clarity lives. Pause is just another way to describe that lost air space we are seeking. Our step back into our own expansive place of sweet and still air allows us to feel the pause. But the reality is that as we start this process, we aren't always going to understand or feel this pause, or find an easy way to step back out of our busy mind. We have been doing this thinking thing for a long time. We may expect to feel this pause right away, but it can be a little elusive. We need to take our expectations in stride.

Often after a meditation I get up and expect to feel something different. And often that doesn't happen. Where was the pause? I am frustrated because I think I should feel peaceful right away. But for some reason I don't. After a fleeting moment of disappointment I stop caring all that much. I have some sort of blind trust in the process. Then out of nowhere a gift is given. Something opens up in me as I am driving to work, walking to the park, or washing the floor, and I am in that pause – that space in between my thoughts. My life just feels lighter and easier somehow. I realize that there is a great spacious opening just below or behind or beside the thought forms. So what does *open up* or *lighter* really mean? Well, for me I always experience these shifts somatically, so I will describe how the pause happens in my body. As I enter the space between thoughts, I feel as though the air in my lungs is taking on a new kind of delicate texture. I have to catch my breath in order to feel the light, tingling sensation in my lungs and the ecstatic wave of air that is winding its way through my chest and finding its way to my fingertips.

Your experience may be a little or a lot different than mine. Proceed with an open mind. Whatever experience you have is unique and worthwhile. And rest assured that your experiences in meditation are absolutely accumulative. You never lose ground. Whatever you learned today is kept in a meditation storage unit for next time. Each experience or seemingly non-experience builds on the other. If you get up after a meditation and think that not much happened, you would be wrong. Imperceptible shifts are going on in the background all the time. With each journey, with each step back we are adding valuable pauses to our lives.

Us and Them

As we step back, we see all kinds of odd things. We notice that there are a bunch of busy thoughts running around with colored markers labeling everything in sight. They are marking everything in groups of two, with names such as up and down, high and low, in and out, good and bad, right and wrong, and so on. These pairs of opposites seem endless. Then we notice that the busy thoughts have drawn a long, straight line with their markers. After a quick look at the line, we see that the pairs of opposites have chosen a side. *Up* picked one side, *down* has chosen the other side. *In* is over here and *out* is over there. All the pairs are sitting on either side of the line, facing each other. Automatically, we are drawn to one side or the other on any given subject, and we can easily get caught up vehemently defending our chosen side. We see how we hold on tightly to our side; how we can get so attached that we become inflexible. We live with the fear of losing what we perceive to be the better side. We have to hold on to our position. In Buddhism, some of these pairs of opposites are described as the eight worldly *dharmas* – pleasure and pain, praise and blame, gain and loss, and fame and disgrace.

A *dharma* is an essential principle or teaching. Understanding these pairs of opposites provides us with some essential teachings. For example, we have positive associations with pleasure, praise, gain and fame. These are things we want and desire. While there is nothing wrong with these per se, it is the grasping and clinging to them that can make us miserable. And it is the attempt to intensify them that can get us into trouble. As for their opposites, we understandably have negative associations with pain, blame, loss and disgrace. These are things we can do without. In an effort to decrease pain or blame, we can easily slide into avoidance, repression and denial. We can get very rigid in our attempts to increase pleasure and decrease pain. This rigidity can affect our quality of life. If we cling too strongly to one side or the other, then we aren't free. Clinging to one of the opposing elements in our lives represents a dual way of thinking that leads to a sense of separate self. If one person is right, then by definition another person has to be wrong. So how do we lessen all of this grasping or avoiding? We go back to the basic principles of watching and stepping back. When we step back and see these goings-on more clearly, we develop a more balanced perspective and we gain a peace and understanding that goes beyond these oppositions.

Attachment

Working with pairs of opposites brings out a sense of attachment. We pick a side, and we know we are right. And in many cases we probably are right – relatively speaking. So the point here is not to criticize our choices but to look at our attachment to these choices. The idea of attachment has often been misinterpreted. Non-attachment doesn't mean that we don't get to pick a particular side. It just means that we aren't all wrapped up in the side we have chosen. We aren't so caught up in our desires that we can't see clearly. Here is a good time to apply *maitri*. When we start to notice how caught we can get on either side of the line, we give ourselves kindness and compassion for our humanness. Through *maitri* we can see the bigger picture and we become a little more neutral about our opinions and the opposing party's opinions.

Remember that neutrality doesn't mean indifference. It just means we aren't holding on for dear life to every opinion or desire that we covet. If a gust of wind comes up, we don't panic and frantically grab for each desire. We let some of them go. In that windy moment, we realize that we don't need to hold on to all of our views of who we are and what we think. We let the wind have some of them. Stepping back helps unlock the rigid thinking that gets stored in the obscure corner of our minds. We become less attached to our coveted views.

Non-attachment also has a relationship with renunciation. Living an austere life, coping with no physical comforts, and meditating all day on a hard surface are not the essence of non-attachment or renunciation. We aren't renouncing certain pleasures because they are inherently bad. We are just looking at how we are attached to certain pleasures, whether physical or emotional. With a new perspective, we strive to renounce those things that ultimately keep us trapped. In stepping back, we are attempting to release some of our attachments, in order to be free. We are renouncing the feeling of being bound, so we can melt away the barriers that keep us from true happiness. In stepping back, we lessen our tendency to see life in terms of good and bad, or us and them.

I had the opportunity to study with a great Zen Master, Thich Nhat Hanh, who teaches internationally, and runs Plum Village, a Buddhist retreat center in southern France. During one of his lectures, Thich Nhat Hanh spoke of an old story from China, about a man going up a river in a small boat.[5] The man is rowing his boat up the river fighting against strong currents, and avoiding protruding rocks. The journey is difficult. As the man is rowing, he looks up and sees another boat coming down the river. He is trying to steer his boat away from the oncoming boat to avoid a collision. But he notices that the other boat doesn't see him, and is coming directly towards his boat. The man starts shouting at the other boat to be careful and not run into him. But it is no use and the other boat collides with his boat, and the man's boat turns over. The man is very angry and he turns to the other boat and starts yelling, *What are you doing? What is wrong with you?* Then as he looks closely, he sees that the other boat is empty. The other boat had been swept down the river by the current, with no driver. Suddenly he isn't angry anymore. His perception, that a person was intentionally doing something to him, was wrong.

We need to step back in order to gain perspective, and not rush to judgment. Our perception about who is wrong and who is right, or who is trying to hurt us and who isn't, can change in an instant with clear seeing.

Where am I Standing?

Stepping back is about changing location. You take a gentle and subtle step back into this sweet empty air space that is vast and limitless. With practice you will recognize its beauty and stillness. Yet, shortly after you have arrived, your air space can get a little crowded. Some tenacious thoughts have been on your trail, and have actually pulled you back to the home base. But you don't always realize this right away. You have to check in over and over again. Ask yourself: *Where am I? Am I really in this new spacious place, or am I just thinking about being in it? Do I need to step back again?* Check it out over and over again, and step back again and again. It's okay because this repetition goes on all of our lives, so we just go with it. With kindness and patience we keep stepping back.

In the Body

We have a lot of thinking going on, all the time. It's everywhere. Thinking runs our lives, and has taken up permanent housing in our heads. So stepping back is about taking a break from thinking. When we took our first imaginary step back, we used the breath as our guide. We followed the rhythm of the breath and stepped back as we exhaled. This focus on breath diverted the mind's attention to the body, where it needs to be. Our body comes in handy because its daily activities are always in the present moment. The body is just doing what it's doing, right now. When we tap into the body presence, we recognize the simplicity of a life without thinking. So we need to go into the body and get physical. The sensation of air moving in and out of our lungs is very physical and tactile, and sensing moving air in the body is a key way to shift out of busy-mind. Visualizing how the breath expands and contracts in the lungs and how the breath can settle into our bones is fascinating. And if our mind rushes in, and we lose track of sensing the breath, then we notice now how thinking feels. We compare the differences between the thinking feeling and the breathing feeling.

Once we are familiar with this difference, we can more easily choose to be in one or the other. Too much of the time, we are in our heads and dissociated from our bodies. When we learn familiarity with the breath, we strengthen our kinship with our physical form. Getting into the breath gets us into our bodies. Getting into our bodies gets us into the present moment.

Counting can help us stay in the body. If I am having trouble keeping my attention on my breath, and where my breath sits in my body, I start counting. I will slowly count to ten, and with each passing number I imagine the strongest physical sensation I can. I count and breathe as if nothing else in the world existed. But this strong sensation has to be created without force. I have to just see myself inside the intensity of counting and sensation as if this intensity already existed, and I just chose to be in it. Big difference. I would count, breathe and feel, again and again. Soon I graduated myself to counting to 20. Sometimes I was able to hold the focus for 20 counts and sometimes I wasn't. Over time, keeping the intensity and getting to 20 became more and more effortless, and I was able to stay truly rooted in my body for longer periods of time.

Bringing our focus into the body can occur in a variety of ways. I often start a meditation class with the breath as the focus. Then I stay open to what ever happens next. For example, a participant in one of my classes could not seem to follow her breath. Alison struggled with the breathing instructions because something was distracting her. She couldn't keep her focus on the inhalation nor the exhalation. Finally, she waved her hand in the air to get my attention. Alison explained that she kept being distracted by a sense of heat running up the left side of her body and into the left side of her neck. Her skin felt as though it was tingling with the heat that was pushing its way through her. It wasn't a good or bad feeling, it was just heat. I said, *"Great, go with it. Use the sensation that exists to find your way into the body. Look at the heat, watch the heat, and perhaps even try to bring your breath into the heat."* Alison was relieved that she could just work with what was, instead of trying to force herself to stay with the exercise. We need to find whatever way we can to move with the breath, or bring the breath to whatever is moving.

Unhinging

Getting into the breath and sensing how it moves through the body can work one day, and then seem impossible the next day. Sometimes, we feel as though our thoughts simply have us, and there is no way out. Our thoughts, worries or fears control us and cloud our vision. So now our way of stepping back has to be more tangible.

On the phone one day, my friend Ann was describing her anxieties and fears about a particular issue in her life. She said she felt consumed by her fear and wasn't sure how to move forward. When I asked if she could try to meditate, she said, "*No, not possible.*" Ann equated meditation with facing her fears head on, and *that* was not what she wanted to do. Ann decided instead that when she felt particularly consumed by fear, she would just do the usual thing, and repress the fear even more. I suggested a new approach. I had Ann draw a stick figure of herself and then draw her fear in or around the drawing. She could draw the fear with any shape, color or size that felt right. Then while holding the drawing in her hands, she would just notice her breath, inhale and do nothing, and then exhale and take an imaginary step back. She would see herself stepping back into the air space of stillness. She would let the air space expand and contract with her breath, allowing the air to be spacious and comforting. If her fear started to follow her into this air space, I asked to her to take another step back and keep separating herself from the emotion lying on the paper.

A week after I had given Ann this suggestion, I called her to see how her attempt at meditation was going. With a surprise in her voice, she said, "*Well, it actually worked! Every time I felt some fear I would open my eyes and look at the piece of paper. Seeing the fear on paper reminded me that my anxiety was not completely consuming me; it was a little removed from me. So then with a sigh of relief, I could go back to noticing my breath. Thanks.*"

Having a strong emotion, such as fear, on paper provides us with a little distance from frightening thoughts. Ann's drawing allowed her to unhinge from the anxiety to separate herself from the fear when she had thought that the two were inseparable. Ann's physical step back was just the short distance between her thoughts and the paper, but her mental step back was immense.

Apart From Pain

This same drawing exercise can also help us get a little distance from physical pain. Just as we did in *Watching*, we start with a pain that is somewhat tolerable. Again we can draw a stick figure of ourselves and then draw the location of the pain in whatever shape, color or size we want. While holding the drawing in our hands, we follow the rhythm of our breath, slowing it down with each exhalation. As we inhale we do nothing. As we exhale, we move the paper a few inches away from our body. As we move the paper away from us, we experience a psychological separation between ourselves and the pain. Our pain can't completely overtake us because it sits in a place that is slightly removed from us. This suggestion of distance from pain is very subtle. But with some creative thinking and a little blind faith, we will start to feel less involved with every little nuance of the pain.

With these smaller somewhat manageable pains, we see that we have some say in how we look at and manage pain. Our helplessness is not inevitable. But if, like Bud, we are dealing with a bigger and more distracting pain, we need more help. We can deal with this bigger pain by softening it around the edges. Bud could draw a much larger version of a pain image – something like a big odd-shaped ball full of various textures and shapes that represented pain. Then he would highlight the outer edge of the ball with a different colored pen. Bud would keep his eye on this outer edge, while taking an imaginary pitcher of water and pouring it over the pain ball. As the water poured down over the ball, Bud would watch and breathe. He would see the colorful, outer edge of the pain image begin to soften and melt. With each tip of the pitcher, the water would erode away a miniscule part of the ball. Then, as the outer edge softened and melted, Bud would notice a slight diminishment in the pain. Bud could keep pouring the water, while looking out for any change in the intensity of pain. With the power of his mind and imagination, Bud could transform the nature, form and strength of the pain.

Testing My Experience

Several years ago I experienced a severe lymphatic swelling in my left arm. My entire arm was swollen and immobile. The pain was intense and relentless. Lying down was impossible because the pain increased if I was even slightly horizontal. So for three nights I sat up on my living room couch stooped over a pile of pillows. Needless to say I had very little sleep for those three nights. The lack of sleep seemed to exacerbate the whole catastrophe. However, during the ordeal there was a small part of me that remained as the witness. At the time I wasn't sure where this ability came from but there it was. I managed to sit just slightly back from the intensity of the pain and watch myself experience the pain.

I can't say that this was easy but I knew that I didn't have much choice because the over-the-counter painkillers didn't seem to help. I had fantasized about going to the hospital and asking for morphine but alas I knew I wouldn't do that. Heavy drugs and I have never been compatible. So there I was – the pillows, the ice pack and me. And I had this curious ability to sit with the pain without freaking out. I knew I was experiencing something new, and this new thing was very much like the feeling I had during deep meditation. I just kept breathing into the pain and watching it and then breathing some more. An understanding of how to cope seemed to arrive out of nowhere. I realized that my meditation practice had in fact been accumulative. A foundation of coping mechanisms had apparently been building up somewhere in my psyche.

A few months after this incident I came across a study in *Science Daily* titled "... Meditation Alleviates Pain, Study Finds". A group of Montreal researchers reported that "... *meditators have lower pain sensitivity both in and out of a meditative state compared to non-meditators*" and that "*slower breathing certainly coincided with reduced pain and may influence pain by keeping the body in a relaxed state.*" The study concluded that "... *meditators experienced an 18 percent reduction in pain intensity.*"[6]

Another study looked at the perception of pain. UNC

Charlotte psychologist, Dr. Fadel Zeidan, has been studying how a single hour of meditation spread out over a three-day period *"can have a positive effect in reducing a person's awareness and sensitivity to pain."* Dr. Zeidan noted that: *"Not only did the meditation subjects feel less pain than the control group while meditating but they also experienced less pain sensitivity while not meditating."*[7]

As you read about these types of studies, you may say what I used to say, *Yes, but that works for other people.* I often said this until I realized I *was* one of those other people. My meditation, as sporadic and unorthodox as it had been at times, had in fact changed my experience with pain. So, take my lead, and dive in to meditation and see what happens to your relationship with pain.

Displacing

In fluid mechanics, displacement occurs when an object is placed in liquid, water for example, and the volume of the object causes the water to rise. As an object descends, the water ascends around the object. With the help of fluid mechanics, we are going to sink down deep like the object, and let rise what rises. We will learn as Ann did that we are not inexorably tied to our thoughts; that our deep inner stillness isn't held captive by the thinking mind. Mind and stillness can live side by side. The concept of displacement can take us far and deep into a felt sense of meditation.

We use our understanding of one object displacing another to experience the unhinging of sticky thoughts. And using water as our medium is easy and familiar. This is because human beings are between 55–65 percent water. Since over half of our body weight is fluid, we can identify with water. In fact, it is fair to say that we are really just these fluid beings warbling around from place to place, ricocheting off of other fluid beings. So with the concept of displacement in mind, we begin to picture the dislodging of tenacious thought patterns. We imagine the smooth and liquid separation of our core self from our thought patterns, remembering that our core self has the wisdom to step back from the endless stream of thoughts and reactions. With displacement, we find a clear division between core self and busy thoughts. The liquid separation, the displacing of one object for another, allows us to unhinge from the busy mind.

We facilitate this separation by focusing on our exhalation. As we breathe out we let our core self sink down into our body and we let our busy mind rise up. With each out breath we, as core self, sink down deeper and deeper. The deeper we go, the more still we become. Displacement occurs in the body, and we settle into sweet relief.

Fixed Emotions

With baby steps, we can also we find our way in and around what I call fixed emotions. These are the emotions that are driven by the tenacious thoughts that stick to us, consume us, depress us, sadden us and annoy us. These emotions are hard, sticky, solid and inflexible. They possess a heaviness that holds us down and keeps us hooked into a story line. The story line can vary according to the scenarios in our lives. *Why did this happen? How did I let this person affect me? Where will I be in the future? What is the point? Why don't things work out according to my plan?* And so on. But these emotions and their story lines are only part of the picture. They are the sticky part. The other part is the witness who recognizes sticky emotions. A simple distinction between the witness of the emotions and the emotions themselves can take us far. Remember the image of two corridors living side by side. This is how sticky and not sticky, heavy and not so heavy, and fixed and not so fixed live.

The corridor full of the solid, fixed emotions can feel like a hard ball of clay similar to the ball of pain that Bud drew. This emotional ball feels fixed and dismal. But there *is* a way to unfix it. We remember that we are essentially water, and with all that

74

water stirring around in us, we can easily imagine moving the emotional ball around a little. As the ball begins to unhinge and shift its position, we understand somatically that the emotional ball is actually less fixed than we thought. Fixed emotions loosen from their sticky positions and rigid mindsets, and begin to bounce around a little. The emotional ball bounces from one side of our body to the other, and bumps up against a few internal walls. The ball is just a part of us that has greater density but needn't necessarily hold us down to one set way of thinking or reacting.

With the loosening of strong fixed emotions, we can again add in the image of pouring water. Anything that holds us can be altered with a little water. Just as Bud did with the pain ball, we pour water over the emotional ball and then watch its outer shell soften as bits and pieces begin to fall away. The more we pour water, the smaller the ball becomes. And even though the reduction in its size is barely perceptibly, the surge of relief that we can actually affect some change in the tenacity of our fixed emotions is huge. So we keep pouring the imaginary water, and we trust that the fixed emotions will simply respond in kind, and ease up. Then when you least expect it, they do.

Now we flip this imagery around. We imagine that *we* are the water that is pouring down over the emotional ball. Remember that we are essentially fluid beings, so this is not that much of a stretch. As we pour ourselves over the ball, we see that we are covering the entire surface of the ball, before running off the sides. As we cascade over the edges, we notice small bits of the ball coming with us. The ball's edges are again softening and unhinging. The little pieces of the fixed emotions are leaving their tightly-packed, protective home and starting to fall away.

This water imagery reinforces the idea that there *is* movement and flexibility when we change the way we see our fixed emotions, and when we find distinctions between *stuck* and *not stuck*. By changing our minds we assist in the shifting and unhinging of seemingly solid and tenacious forms. The once tight form of an emotion can now be seen as a kind of non-form. We can find breathing space and welcome relief where we thought there was none.

With this next visualization, we let the breath make a distinction between form and non-form, and between up and down, in order to find our way in.

Teeter-Totter

With your breath
You can do anything
You can make up seem like down
And down seem weightless
You can separate the inseparable
You can find thought
And fall into no thought

With your breath
You can begin the process
Of separating busy from still
Of detaching full from empty
Of letting one side fall
So the other can rise
Breath rising
Breath falling

As you breathe in
Thoughts rise and stillness falls
As you breathe out
Thoughts fall and stillness rises
The very act of falling
Gives way to rising
One displacing the other

Moving up and down
Thought and no thought
Brushing by each other
Thick with purpose
Thought unhinges
From its own weight
And no thought discovers
The sweet ache of stillness
With the rising and falling
With the coming and going

The quiet you
Sinks into a spaciousness
Unknown to your skin and bones
You crawl into this stillness
With eyes closed
And breath deep

With the rising and falling
You now feel a lightness
That is expansive and supple
Air moves through you now
Waves of weightlessness
Let you rest

With the rising and falling
With the coming and going
You are full then empty
You are busy then still
One replacing the other
With your breath
You can do anything

Our Journey

We have learned to step back, and then step back again, and fall away and then fall away again. Remembering that the repetitive nature of our journey is accompanied by *maitri*, we don't need to panic if we lose our way. With kindness, we just try again – no big deal.

Falling away is just releasing back into some sweet air space. Once we sense that there *is* a roomy air space to step back into, and that there *is* a way to allow breath to create some room, we can rest easy and let out a big sigh of relief. We can let our tightly bound world collapse a little, and let our rigid holding of the mind melt into something new and curious. We remember that we left town and stepped back for a reason. We left behind those meandering streets, predictable twists and turns, and hard-coded thought patterns, and found a new way.

In stepping back, we didn't try to annihilate our thought process, but we strengthened something else instead – something other than thought. Stepping back allowed us to see our *other* selves; the selves that we didn't remember. This newfound core self isn't a projection of a thought, or a manifestation of an idea. It's just us. Now that we have seen what is possible, it is time to step in.

Chapter Four

Stepping In

Now we are ready to go back home. We turn ourselves around, and head back into town. Our old town seems smaller somehow but there is a sweetness in the air, and we can see folks in their yards, waving us in. We inhale and pause. We exhale and step in.

We're back in town to participate in our own lives. We are ready to walk the streets, observe the mind patterns and just be present. We are committed to living in the middle of our busy ways, the dutiful rights and wrongs, and the notions of good and bad. Our town can heat us up and cool us down. It can toss us back and forth; no matter. We move *with* the chaos, and we stay very still. We see that both chaos and stillness can happen at the same time, and that we are right in the middle, staying awake, and everything is all right. We are just there breathing, in the only moment there is.

Facing our thoughts, our fears and our selves is not so daunting now. We know that we are stepping in from solid ground. We are prepared to face whatever needs to be faced. We have stabilized our minds, and we have learned that our thoughts don't really have us. They are just young children running around making a lot of noise and trying to get our attention. We also have some compassion for this busy mind. It has a lot of important things to do and say. But the expansive air space in which we can rest allows us to breathe, see and feel the quiet in the midst of it all.

Now that we are back in town, we notice the proverbial large, gray, floppy-eared mammal in the middle of the street. This big form is full of thoughts, opinions and fears, and it is just standing in the middle of the street, apparently unnoticed. The townspeople are doing everything they can to avoid seeing or running into this beast. Worries and unwanted thoughts are not on their agenda for today, and the townspeople are just simply too busy doing *other* things. Besides, they just want to have a nice day, for crying out loud. They don't *want* to talk or think about this and that right now. Ho-hum, ho-hum, they sing, as they walk down the street taking a slightly circuitous route. Ho-hum.

Then we come along and sit right down on the pavement and look straight at the elephant. We've wrecked their plan. The other people may not want to deal with this right now. But we do. So we sit and look at the details in front of us – gray skin, long trunk, dense muscle, intense eyes. We feel a sweet sadness in this immense form. The other people watch us pet this beast, and watch us feel its pulse and purpose. They see us touch the under-belly and not disappear or get swallowed up. We just settle down beside the elephant, the two of us coexisting.

We don't need to get rid of the elephant or the heavy mind form. Our awareness now holds a wisdom that can go right inside form and then beyond it. When we look right at the thoughts and fears, we see that they aren't that unusual or strange. They are somewhat ordinary musings that have been infused with a lot of charge. Our awareness diffuses that charge, and lets the thoughts go back to being ordinary and not so fright-ening. And right here is when we remember that we are capable of the extraordinary. We are just beginning to tap into our ability for limitless expansion. The extraordinary is in us, and all around us. We only have to settle in and let it happen.

The Delicious Middle

Right in the center is where we want to be – not straining to see what might happen, not looking over our shoulder at what has happened. We rest in the center experiencing, watching and feeling all our comings and goings. We have heard catch phrases such as *accept, surrender,* or *let go.* Whatever these have meant for other people or other disciplines, we start right now to define these terms for ourselves, in whatever way we can imagine. We sit in the middle of the pleasant and the unpleasant. We stay in the center of worries, thoughts, problems, emotions, hurts, or stresses – just as they are. If we resist our issues then their knots and tangles get tighter. So we let them move around us, brush up against us, and still we remain with no struggle.

With this next visualization, our goal is not to transcend thoughts and emotions. Our goal is just to be with them. Let yourself settle into a seat of stillness at the water's edge.

Buddha in the Water

Feeling the rhythm of your breath
You follow your feet
To the water's edge
Warm sand moving under you
As your feet find the water
You take your rightful seat
At the place where sand and water meet

Sitting like a Buddha
Still and quiet
With water moving around you
And soft sand beneath you
You sit in stillness
You hold your ground
No words are needed
You sink in to your seat
Still and quiet

Small waves touch you
Warm water moves around you
Calling you

Asking you
To think, to be amused
To be distracted
Water brushes up against you
Wanting your attention
Your body knows this water
Has felt this sand
But your body, like a Buddha
Holds the stillness

Water swirls around you
Water nudges against you
And you stay... you notice
And you breathe
Your breath fills you up
Your breath keeps you still
Your stillness is greater
Than the water has known
Small waves brush against you
Again and again
But you are a Buddha
Holding the stillness

You stay... and you breathe
Only stillness
Only breath
The small waves are back
They touch you with their questions
Their longing and their fears
But you stay

You stay for all those who are taken away
By the seduction of the water
By the rhythm of distraction

You are not moved by the waves
Not taken by the water
You live in your state of grace
In your being
In the stillness
Of your seat
Where sand and water meet

You continue to recognize that you can sustain a stillness that is anchored and comfortable. The comings and goings of busy-mind patterns become less and less distracting as your focus on breath and stillness increases.

Using Whatever We Have

Learning to stay in simple focus means we take whatever creative leaps we can. Our creativity can build a meditation practice that is appealing and easy. We have enough struggles in our lives without adding more, so we find ways to use whatever we have around us to our advantage. Let's take noises for example. A barking dog, a cawing crow or the tick of a clock all have their ways of distracting or irritating us. But if we learn to move into the sound rather than just hear the sound, we change the way we experience noise. We can focus in on a particular sound that is distracting or irritating us and imagine it as a sound wave with a particular size and shape. The wave could be tall, short, dense, spacious, thick or thin. We watch the sound wave as it enters our body, moves through our ears, and lands in some obscure location in our body. We start to track exactly where the sound wave is going and how it feels. Now here is the tricky part. We reverse our thinking. We make a decision that this sound could be helpful. I know that sounds impossible, especially if our sound is particularly irritating, but it is oddly possible. Focusing on its texture and power, we find a way to make the sound useful. We climb inside the sound and see what we can use. We imagine that the wave's rough edges are useful and even comforting. We imagine that the power of the sound wave actually creates some space in us, and that our breath can widen into this new space. Then we can crawl inside the new space and take a look around.

Let your imagination have its own way with this imagery, and then see what unfolds. When you notice a slight change in the way you perceive a sound, take note. Explore the ways in which this sound might be useful. Then your mind will probably interrupt you and say, *But this noise is bothering me*, over and over again. Then you come in and say, *This noise could be useful*, over and over again.

Starting with a consistent sound or white noise is easier because it is less disruptive. You can ride the wave of white noise by allowing it to move through your body. If you don't have a consistent white noise, you should seek one out. A fan or a heater can work because they have an even sound. This even sound of white noise starts to represent the present moment, if you climb inside it deeply enough. Eventually you hear the present moment within the sound. The texture of the present moment becomes so thick you can feel it on your skin and in your bones.

For me, this experiment with white noise took some getting used to. But I did learn to let the noise deepen my meditation rather than let it drive me away. I started with a simple white noise, the sound of the little heater at my feet. I used the consistent even noise to remind me of the consistency of my breath.

I found where the noise and my breath could meet. They seemed to be working together to help my lungs expand and contract as I breathed. I started welcoming the sound as a useful tool to keep me focused on my breath. The heater noise would keep bringing me back to my breath right then, so it provided a reference point and an anchor for the present moment.

Using Other Sounds

After some time with the white noise, you can bravely venture into the world of intermittent noises – a lot trickier. Lawnmowers, the plane overhead, the tapping on a keyboard or the resonance of a dog bark all have a texture that can be felt. Finding your way into these sounds requires creative thinking. Use color, sensation, and images, and make it up as you go along. With practice, I was able to wait for the intermittent sound, catch it and ride on its wave. I practiced welcoming each individual wave as if I had invited it. Remember, we tell ourselves that this *is* possible, and then we allow our imaginations to find a way to make it work. We become more tolerant of our environment, and we realize that we can meditate anywhere. We use whatever is happening in the moment as an opportunity to be awake and mindful. In a split second, the seemingly impossible can transform into something doable.

Doing what seems impossible points to the power of the mind. This wonderful, mostly-untapped resource sitting inside our skull has so much to offer. Scientists often talk about the power of the mind to affect healing in a patient. Think of the placebo phenomenon. There have been many reported cases of patients getting better because they believe they are receiving a particular treatment or drug even though they are not. They have a subjective perception of a therapeutic effect, which causes them to feel as if their condition has improved. This placebo effect points to the power of perception and the immense ability of the mind to affect physical change.

My own experience of the mind's power came when I was pregnant with my daughter. I was 30 weeks in, and had ten more weeks to go. Sadly though, my body collapsed in some mysterious way, and my water broke at 30 weeks. The hospital staff informed me, very solemnly, that babies born at 30 weeks are high risk and will experience a plethora of health issues. I was also told that there was a 99.8 percent chance that I would go into labor within 48 hours. All the staff could do at that point was to monitor me and hope for the best. But in a mother-bear manner I asked if it was possible to not go into labor after 48 hours. They repeated their statistics stating that it was next to impossible. I persisted. *What does next to impossible mean? Had it ever been done before? Had anyone passed the dreaded 48 hour mark?* Dr. Leigh, the obstetrician on duty, said he had heard of one case in which a woman went several weeks without going into labor, but that it was very rare.

That was enough for me. My decision was made. With great resolve and raw instinct, I closed the door of my hospital room, put a do-not-disturb sign on the door, and started meditating for my life, or rather for my daughter's life. At that point in time, I had only been practicing meditation, on and off, for maybe a few months. But I knew enough. I somehow knew that my resolve and clear intention would hold this baby in for a least four more weeks. Dr. Leigh had told me that if a baby can get to at least 34 weeks, then all of the major organs and neurological systems would be developed enough for the baby to survive on its own. Even the sucking reflex would be ready by 34 weeks. So that was my goal. Seal this baby inside me with rich imagery, white light and pure intention for four more weeks, minimum.

The door was closed, my room was my own and my child was my focus. I was very present and motivated with this mission. Nothing distracted me from the goal. I loved my meditations and visualizations because I knew they were saving my child. Throughout the days, I would use my breath, and the blue sky and soft clouds out my window as my meditation assistants. They helped my daughter and I fly around, taking imaginary flights of fancy without cares or worries. We were two flying shapes of light that felt weightless and free.

The first week passed without incident. My room became a haven of soft lighting, dried flowers, Gregorian chants, and healthy snacks brought in by family and friends. Dr. Leigh came in to check on me. He said, *"Whatever you are doing, keep doing it!"* No problem there, and back we went into the blue sky flying through cool, welcoming clouds.

The second week went pretty much the same way. More good food, more music and more flying. By the third week, Dr. Leigh started to look puzzled. He came to the side of my bed and sat down. *"Do you know that what you are accomplishing here is very rare, almost unheard of? What is it exactly that you are doing?"* I look at him in a rather matter-of-fact way and said, *"I am meditating."* He looked surprised, and leaned in a little closer and asked, *"Can you tell me about meditation?"* So I did. We discussed the matter for a few minutes before he had to continue his rounds. Dr. Leigh left with pretty much the same puzzled look he had come in with.

By the fourth week, I had some nurses asking if they could sit in my room during their 15 minute breaks, so they could relax a little. The soft chanting, the beauty of the flowers and apparently my demeanor seemed to calm them. The whole four weeks were full of my absolute resolve that nothing was going to cause my body to go into labor. I had been told many times and I knew myself that I must get to at least 34 weeks. My mind was made up and it seemed to have the power to stay made up. My focus was steady and comforting – 34 weeks, 34 weeks. It was like a mantra.

Then the day came when I hit the 34 week mark, to the day. I had come in to the hospital on a Sunday and it was exactly four Sundays later that I realized I had reached my goal. I had somehow used the power of my mind and my mother-bear intention to save this baby from a life of health issues. My mind made the decision that my body needed to hold on for four weeks, and my body complied. With daily meditations, of my own kooky design, I held on. In fact, as I look back now, I realize that I was probably in a continuous state of meditation for the whole four weeks.

Right at the moment that I felt the safety net of reaching 34 weeks, I released my intention. And guess what? I went right into labor. Seven hours later, my daughter was born healthy and strong at a meager four pounds. After only a few days of observation and feeding assistance, we went home.

My baby story is told here to illustrate the power of the mind – a power I had no idea I had. And likely a power that you may have no idea you have. But there it is. If I had heard this story from someone else, I would have said the usual thing to myself about how these kinds of amazing events happen to *other* people. It turns out that I *was* other people. And with the help of tools such as meditation, we are all *other* people – people getting a glimpse into what is possible with the mind. The possibilities now abound. We can find ways to handle difficult situations, or impending crises with an inspired belief in our own mind's abilities. We can even learn to tolerate physical pain in a new way.

Inside Pain

At the gas station that morning I heard and saw how pain affected Bud. As I watched him lay his hand on his chest, I knew that his physical experience of pain dominated his life. And his eyes spoke of his need for help. Bud's understanding of meditation had been somewhat limited, but he had a sense that some relief may lie in this notion of calming the mind and moving inward. Bud's experience of pain resonates with our human experience of pain. We are all looking for a way out, or *in* as the case may be. Meditation can allow us to handle pain in a new way. As we practice stepping in, we learn to move inside of pain. Don't worry; this is not as painful as it sounds. We aren't stepping in so we can experience more pain. We are just learning to create some air space inside the discomfort. The constrictive nature of physical pain needs some breathing room.

Toning

To create some room inside of pain, we experiment with various sounds of our own making. We start off with a big sigh, and imagine flopping back into a big, cushy chair. We think of ending a long day of work as we let out our sigh. The sound that we let out of our body is long and breathy. With each sigh, we lengthen the sound that we make. The tone feels gentle and slow, and it symbolizes relief. After each full breath in, we let the out-breath carry our tone for as long as it can. We do this a few minutes a day to become familiar with our tone.

Extending your sigh on the out-breath is known as toning. We use toning to work with physical pain. With our tone, we move right into the area of discomfort. We allow the wave of sound from the tone to wind its way through the tightness and constriction of pain. As we ride on the crest of the sound wave we find our way in. Then our tone moves inside the pain and creates some room, some *breathing* space. The toning allows air to move inside of pain.

I used toning when I was in labor with my daughter. I didn't know beforehand that I would even think to use it, but somehow a part of me knew how and when to apply this tool. With each contraction, I would tone whatever sound came to me and let the sound continue until the end of the contraction. I took myself right to the crest of the sound wave and rode it all the way through the minute or so of pain. By riding the wave I was essentially moving with the pain rather than pushing against it. I understand now that I was drawing on the strengthened habit of practicing toning and experimenting with staying focused on a sound. I must have also inadvertently been building up a trust in the process of stepping inside of the thing I wanted to avoid. This trust allowed me to be curious about the pain as though I could live inside it and handle it. I was coexisting with the phenomenon of pain. Sound, air and spaciousness moved in to replace the tightness and fear contained in the pain.

As you experiment with sound, try not to get too structured with the process. You can change the tone or vary its length. Just be willing to see what works for the particular pain you have. If sometimes you find that making a sound requires too much effort or focus, then just stay with the breath. You can imagine that you are making a tone on the out-breath without actually making an audible sound. Whether you make a sound or not, the breath is always your foundation. It is the eternal sweet return that allows you to navigate your way through pain.

How We See It

While running errands one day, I heard a song on the radio by Joni Mitchell. There was a line in the song that caught my attention – *"laughing and crying, you know it's the same release."*[8] I thought, *Huh, that is so true*. There are common traits in both these emotions. They have a similar intensity, they have a familiar ache, their charge sits in the same part of the body, and they affect our breathing in the same way. Yet we look at these two emotions very differently. We want to laugh, and we don't want to cry. We want the good, and we don't want the bad. Our pairs of opposites elicit our judgment about what is desirable. I want this and I don't want that. We are wrapped up in the comings and goings of emotions, and all of their story lines. We perceive our emotions as well formed in their individual identities with no fluidity, no room for movement.

But as we learn to sit in the middle of our emotions, we can see the whole situation differently. We recognize that the physical nature of our pairs of opposites is essentially the same. Laughing and crying have the same electric charge once we put aside the story that accompanies them. So we use this charge as a kind of raw energy that can suit our purposes. We allow the electricity of the charge to facilitate an expansion of our awareness. We see our emotions becoming more fluid and flexible. We simply adjust our thinking, and recognize that this raw energy can pave the way to that lost air space; that place of unencumbered existence. Adjusting our thinking holds an opportunity. We have no need to be completely caught in whether we are laughing or crying, because those singular emotions no longer grab us in the same way.

In this next visualization emotions and thoughts blend together into one useful energy source; the charge inside the charge, like water inside of water.

Water to Water

A drop of water falls
Meeting the still pond below
Cascading downward
You watch the falling
And you begin to feel
Feel the sensation
Of the returning
Water to water

As the drop of water meets the pond
You begin to feel the sensation
Of the expanding
Water greeting water
You feel the ripples and waves
And your body gives way
Opening and welcoming
Water to water

Wave after wave
Opening wider and wider
Ripple after ripple
You give way
To an expansion

That lives
Beyond your beliefs
Beyond your thoughts

You become the expansion
Reaching further and further
And dissolving into ripples
Water inside of water

A drop of water
And your mind gives way
Releases its grip
Releasing inward
Ripple after ripple
Opening, breathing, not minding
Thoughts blending into thoughts
Mind dissolving into water
The melting of form
The transformation of thought

Determination is slippery now
Conviction gives up its hold
You and the endless ripples
Opening
Breathing
Returning
Water to water

Seeing our emotions and reactions fold into themselves and transform into a new source of energy is inspiring. We *can* turn things around. We *can* take our mind and our reactions and set them to a new frequency by rearranging the way we experience our world.

Changing It Up

We know that the mind gets used to its own version of reality. It is comfortable knowing that sounds are to be heard, sensations are to be felt, and sights are to be seen. This knowing runs deep. But why not short-circuit this predictable thinking pattern? One day during a meditation, I inadvertently changed the circuits in my mind. I started hearing the heat from my heater, seeing the sound of the fan, and feeling the light in the room. My senses did this strange and interesting flip. My bearings changed and I felt as though my mind could now disperse its hold, go into unfamiliar territory and then completely let go, for a split second. The whole circuit change felt very freeing, so I decided to incorporate this experience into my regular meditation practice. I would intentionally try to flip my senses around. The more I did this flip, the more anchored I became in the moment.

One spring afternoon, I walked to the bottom of the stairs at Trafalgar Street and looked out at waves, seaweed, rocks and kayaks. As I took in my surroundings, I felt a curious shift in my perceptions. I suddenly felt as though I could taste the sounds around me, and hear the texture of the water. My senses felt differently wired. A beach walker passed in front of me and I watched how his body moved with each step. He probably had no idea that as he placed each foot down on the sand, I could hear and feel a rhythmic drum sound move through me. In my mind, he was actually dancing as he walked. And as I watched him *dance*, I felt deeply anchored to the present moment. I realized that this acute awareness of the present moment was everywhere all the time. This moment was wider and higher than a linear time line, and it was beyond definition. I embraced every millisecond of this experience so I could know it as a sweet memory. I have learned that these heightened states of awareness are to be appreciated and released. Clinging or yearning wouldn't bring them back. There wasn't much point in hoping for this experience to return just as it was, because it wouldn't. So I could save my breath and look forward to how the next experience would *not* be like the previous one. In so doing, my expectations wouldn't limit my appreciation of the next moment.

What I learned on my walk that day was not to fear the experience of rewired sensations. When I could see the waves of sound coming from the seagulls, or feel the quiet as a tangible presence in my chest, or eat the time that lay ahead of me, I was intrigued. And as always, I tried to suspend the objections of the thinking mind, for I was trying to create something new and unpredictable that would take me to a place I didn't yet know. And the unpredictable kept on coming.

Rearranging the Elements

During a regular meditation sitting, sneaky and tenacious thoughts kept, as usual, entering my mind. How insistent and familiar they were. I was annoyed with them. I must have forgotten about acceptance and simple watching. Amnesia runs rampant in the world of meditation. The thoughts seemed to be in control. My health was the main focus of the thought patterns – same old circular ideas about how to heal, how to feel strong again, how to get it right, and so on. Suddenly, my mind kind of popped and said, *Enough! Simply enough.* I guess I had had enough and I was asking for a change. I checked to see if it felt like I was demanding a change and or just deciding that something had to change. Was this a push or just a decision? It was the latter.

The decision to have it be enough moved through my body like a foreign substance. And carried on that substance was the word reconfigure. Where did that come from? I never use that word. Reconfigure. There it was again. Then all of the molecular structures around my body or in my body – I am not really sure – reconfigured themselves. I know, sounds strange. It was strange and amazing at the same time. It was as though I was one of those yogis you hear about who can affect physical changes in their bodies. Not that I felt as far out as those yogis but I did reconfigure something. And in my reconfiguration – I am still enjoying the novelty of this word – all the old thought patterns about my health stopped, or vanished or simply reconfigured. I guess I could say the molecules in and around me rearranged themselves. The sensation I had was profoundly different than anything I had felt before.

The molecular formation I was left with felt like complete balance or full alignment. The moment was uplifting and encouraging. It seems that for those few seconds I had the ability to change physical form by altering my experience of my thoughts. I am not sure if I can fully describe the experience in words, but there it was – reconfiguration!

Immediately after the experience was over I said to myself, as any good human would, *Will it happen again?* Expectation is always quick to settle in. So the next time I sat down to meditate I just let the expectations have their way. I let my mind ask, *Is this it? Is it happening again? Is this it?* Once I got past the questions, I began to notice a different sensation in the meditation. I felt almost cavernous as I watched my breath. I was breathing in some kind of unfettered space. So much so, that I felt the need to cling to the walls of the vast space because I wasn't sure of my footing. The meditation almost seemed undisciplined. Not that disciplined is a word I would use to describe my meditations in the first place, but undisciplined seemed to be the right word for this experience. My new cavern was unruly in a delightfully yet cautious way.

From that point on, my meditations did feel a little different in an intriguing way, but months did go by without any more reconfigurations. So, I just pondered the word reconfiguration and waited to see if more understanding would arrive, or not. Either way.

A few months after the initial reconfiguration, I decided that I wanted to experiment with the concept again. How should I start? Should I repeat the circumstances from the previous experience? Should I set an intention? Should I simply try to make it happen? None of this worked. So I just sat on my bed and started noticing my breath. *Right! Good place to start.* Breathing, wondering, and watching filled some time. Then I thought that instead of chasing the state of reconfiguration I could imagine that the state lived just back from where I was sitting. Floating around in its only little sphere could be a place where molecules or particles or whatever just started rearranging themselves into a state of wellness and stillness. Why not? I decided to go with the idea that this could perhaps exist. Then on an exhalation I imagined that I was falling back into this place. Not falling in a dramatic sense, but falling in a light, barely perceptible sense. It worked. I felt that same odd feeling of internal rearranging, and my body became very still and started to feel whole. Not that my body hadn't been physically whole before, but this was a new sense of completeness and balance. For someone who has dealt with minor physical challenges her entire life, I felt the sense of completeness, balance and wholeness as a welcome relief. Somehow I felt as though my mind or brain had the capacity to alter itself or expand into an area it hadn't used before.

I had read about the plasticity of the brain in a science journal and it made be wonder. Could my grey matter be improved, increased or changed by meditation? I came across an article in which researchers at Harvard, Yale and the Massachusetts Institute of Technology "*... found the first evidence that meditation can alter the physical structure of our brains. Brain scans they conducted reveal that experienced meditators boasted increased thickness in parts of the brain that deal with attention and processing sensory input.*" Furthermore, their "*data suggest that meditation practice can promote cortical plasticity in adults in areas important for cognitive and emotional processing and well-being.*"[9]

Reconfiguration landed in my lap and I continue to ponder its purpose and abilities. And as usual, if I go looking for it with intensity and fervor, it reveals its elusive quality. The reconfiguration experiment continues.

As always, the question arises as to how these kinds of experiences fit into our regular lives. How could I use the experience of reconfiguring? Waiting and watching was the way to go. I would just keep showing up each day, and sit in my boat and watch the breath. Maybe I won't ever reconfigure again. Maybe you will reconfigure, but it will look completely different. I don't know what is *supposed* to happen for anyone, or for me, for that matter. All I can encourage you to do is just sit in your boat and see what happens. Best not to plan, just show up and watch your meditations take on a life of their own.

Moving Around

Meditation doesn't have to be separate from the rest of our lives. We often will do a meditation practice and then carry on with our regular lives; *this* practice, then *that* life. But really *this* can live inside of *that*. No matter where we are, *this* and *that* can work together. In the same way that we settle into our old town, we start working from within; incorporating our newfound sense of presence into our daily world. Many of you have heard of walking meditation, in which the sensation of walking becomes the focus. Feeling each step anchors your awareness to the moment. Now we are going to add a new twist to walking meditation.

Instead of focusing on each footstep, I like to pick a wall that I can run my hands along. As I close my eyes and slowly walk along the wall, I feel for texture and temperature, bumps or crevices. I think of the wall as something that occupies space, and contains a mass of molecules and particles moving at a certain speed. I let the skin of my hands interpret the wall's density and property. Then I run my hands across a doorframe and a doorknob, making note of the change in texture, temperature and density. If I come across an open doorway, I make note of the spacious, less dense property of air.

This has become my moving meditation. Each day, on my way out the door, my hand reaches for the doorknob and I make a mental note, *Ah doorknob – slippery assembly of atoms with a constant density.* As I stroll in the rain, I say, *Ah water – cool liquid with variable density.* As I walk down the sidewalk, I say, *Ah concrete – inert matter with tightly-packed particles.* As I encounter a friend, I say, *Ah friend – warm mass with 50 trillion cells producing energy, and exchanging information.*

We are building our awareness of the matter and density of objects and non-objects around us. The more tactile our relationship with our environment, the more mindful we become of our every step and movement. As we bring our skin into contact with non-skin objects, we develop an acute sensitivity to what is going on around us. Become familiar with the textures in your life. Every thing or person we come in contact with is a reminder for us to be mindful of right now. Mindfulness is our focus as we bring our practice into everyday life.

The textures and fluidity of the objects and people around us begin to teach us that there is nothing all that solid about our world. And without a solid difference between *us and them*, we start to see separateness slip away. When Dr. Jill Bolte Taylor experienced a shift in perception after a stroke to her left hemisphere, she wrote "... *without the judgment of my left brain saying that I am solid, my perception of myself returned to this natural state of fluidity. Clearly, we are each trillions upon trillions of particles in soft vibration. We exist as fluid-filled sacs in a fluid world where everything exists in motion.*" Dr. Bolte Taylor went on to say "... *I was not capable of experiencing separation or individuality. Despite my neurological trauma, an unforgettable sense of peace pervaded my entire being and I felt calm.*"[10]

A Closer Look

When we look at the cells, particles and density of the objects around us, we begin to understand that matter is relative. An object or our skin or the rain is just as dense as or less dense than anything else. We can imagine that thoughts have density as well. An intense thought would be thick and slow moving, and a lighter thought would be airy and fast moving. We can view all of these thoughts, moving around in our heads, as just various types of matter. Whether we are happy, disturbed, pensive or gleeful, our thought patterns provide their own interesting particle formations.

As always, we remember that no matter what density our thoughts manifest, we absolutely are still breathing. Our thread of breath winds its way through even the densest of mind patterns. Breath is tenacious and travels through pretty much anything. We can imagine our thread of breath navigating its way through busy thinking. If thoughts are strong and dense, we can see the thread as rather thin and wiry. It has very little room as it winds its way through our body and mind. If thoughts are light and airy, our breath thread becomes more expansive and flexible. It can easily travel in, around, under and over our collection of thought particles. The thread's characteristics change from day to day, from situation to situation.

The thread of breath image becomes very useful when we are stuck in dense reaction patterns. Earlier we talked about the thoughts that have a lot of power and want to hold on tight: the ones with a lot of *shenpa*. These thoughts cause our thread to become thinner and tighter. But then we remember that the thread has the ability to expand to great proportions once it finds some space between the particles. We can use the power of our breath and imagination to find this expansion.

Using our thread of breath as our ally, we can play with our thoughts. We can gently shake up their patterns and alter their structure. The shifting of formations and the moving of particles can happen because we now see clearly that all matter is just a collection of particles with variable density – including thoughts.

And a collection of particles can always move, even just a little.

If we look at water or a rock or even our skin under a microscope we will see that these objects are not as solid as we think. There are thousands of moving molecules that represent these seemingly solid objects. We realize that solidity is essentially an illusion, both with matter and with our thoughts.

More Motion

All particles in matter move all of the time, and movement itself has infinite possibilities. Sustained movement is a great tool for cultivating acute awareness. When we are moving in a continuous rhythm as in running, cycling, rocking or dancing, the consistency of motion can take us beyond the structure of linear thought. Runners talk about getting into the zone or dancers describe the point where the dance takes over. Rocking a baby to sleep is calming and transformative.

Consistent movement frees us up to experience something beyond movement, and beyond form and thought. It allows us to slip into the air space that resonates with non-thought. We can lose ourselves – our thinking selves – in the essence of motion. As we did in *Drinking Water*, we watch for the moment when we aren't dancing or running or even breathing in a left brain linear way but we are suddenly being danced or being run or being breathed. We can also feel a sensation of being walked when we experiment with different types of walking meditations. I like to find new ways to ground through my feet when I do a walking meditation.

Down Through the Feet

When I spoke at my father's funeral, I became very familiar with my feet. Anchored to the wooden planks of the chapel floor were these two appendages of mine, covered in soft black-leather shoes. When I talked about my father, my words seemed to resonate inside my body, and then run down through my feet. I was wondering if these words carried sound, and could be understood. Based on the nodding and sympathetic faces in the pews, my words must have been heard.

I was talking about my father. I was feeling my feet. And I was anchored in the moment. The air in my lungs and the muscles in my throat produced my speech, but the words seemed to belong to my feet, and I was thankful. More than anything, I needed to be rooted into that moment.

When the service was over, I was directed to walk down a long, carpeted aisle to the back of the chapel. But before I could stand up from the pew, I had to convince my feet to comply. They seemed to need some prompting and instructions as to how we were going to take this walk. I started visualizing the walk as a kind of virtual stepping meditation. I looked down the aisle and visualized my right foot and then my left foot taking slow deliberate steps toward the back of the chapel. I planned to have my virtual feet go first, defining the route, and then have my real feet slide into the spots that were mapped out for them. My feet agreed and off we went. Step by step, we walked both virtually and actually down the aisle. My slow deliberate stepping meditation got me to the back of the chapel.

A few weeks later, I was walking down the hall in my house and I remembered this stepping meditation. I decided to incorporate the idea of virtual steps, followed by real steps, into the traditional walking meditation. I stood at one end of the hall, and took some slow deep breaths. Then I imagined my right foot stepping forward, followed by my left foot. They each took virtual turns stepping forward. Down the hall they went – one virtual foot after the other.

When my virtual feet got to the end of the hallway, I could see clearly the path they had mapped out for me. So I let my real right foot slide into the first footprint left by my virtual right foot. The left foot then followed suit. I walked my real feet to the end of the hall, sliding into each footprint, deeply anchoring me in the walking meditation. By visualizing the placement of each foot ahead of time, I reinforced the feeling of complete presence in the moving meditation.

Some days though, my virtual walking meditation needed to be more tangible. A more tactile sense of the steps mapped out for me was called for. So I took a large piece of cloth and cut out ten footprints in the shape of my foot. I then laid these ten cloth feet all the way down the hallway in a typical walking pattern. Stepping onto each cloth footprint easily helped me stay focused. The sense of fabric on my bare feet anchored me to each particular footprint.

You can try this anywhere. Simply find a place to send your virtual feet, or your cloth feet, walking ahead of you. Then as you step into the footprints mapped out for you, feel yourself becoming deeply anchored in the present moment.

Any type of movement meditation keeps us grounded in the body. And the more familiar we become with our body, the more connected we become with our emotions. For better – but sometimes it feels for worse – we are moving inside our bodies and minds to feel and hear exactly what is there.

Doing the Opposite

Most often, when we feel our own anguish, pain or fear we want to push it away. We feel it would best if our issues could just evaporate. But instead we are going to try something that is counterintuitive. We are going to breathe in our pain. *Tonglen* is the Tibetan word for this process of pulling in a difficult emotion. I see *Tonglen* as the homeopathy of meditation practice because we take in exactly what we see as the problem. Pema Chodron describes this practice as *"using poison as medicine."*[11]

With *Tonglen*, we breathe in everything that frightens or worries us. We breathe it in for ourselves and for the human condition. We do this in order to expand our view of the world, and awaken compassion for our own and for other people's suffering. With *Tonglen* we learn to use the breath to dissolve any tightness in our hearts, and move past excessive self-interest. On the inhalation we embrace the weighty and the dark, we transform it, and then we breathe out relief. With the help of the breath, we absorb our pain and the pain of those around us, and change it into something we can work with. Sounds like a tall order, so we start simply.

I start by imagining an issue in my life that is not too huge to bear, perhaps a disappointment that I recently had. I breathe in the feeling of disappointment and let it settle into my body. As I breathe in the emotion, I give it a texture and color, and then I watch the texture and color change and lighten as it moves through my body. I breathe in this feeling so it can dissipate and lose its charge. As I exhale, I breathe out relief and ease, and a new texture and color for the emotion. The disappointment is transformed into relief, as it rides the wave of my breath. The image of the relief sitting on the crest of this breath wave is accessible and intriguing. Imagery of any sort can be our most helpful tool.

To understand the feeling of *Tonglen*, I visualize a large empty house inside of me. My house has open windows and light-colored walls. The walls are translucent and flexible, and they can expand endlessly. The walls can hold structure in order to define non-structure. Anything can fit into my house for it can accept any of the thoughts outside, inside, beside and around it. My house's capacity is so great that it can eat up my pain and suffering, transform the heavy to light, and deliver ease and relief. *Tonglen* is the compassionate transformer that lives in my house.

We can use *Tonglen* to arouse compassion for people we know and love. As we breathe in fear, for example, we recognize that someone we know feels this same fear. As we take in pain, we recall that someone very close to us feels this same pain. So we breathe in the suffering of a friend, convert it within ourselves, and then breathe out a sense of ease for this friend. We breathe in the pain of a loved one, imagine their pain dissipating and then breathe out relief on their behalf. Just the intention or hope to transform suffering of any kind gives us an active role in healing.

Also, we can do *Tonglen* for people we *don't* know. We expand our practice to include the suffering of our fellow humans. In Buddhism, the first noble truth is that there is suffering. We recognize that suffering exists all over the world. This is a very large truth. With *Tonglen*, we walk in someone else's shoes, and we are reminded that we are not alone. We breathe in the larger pains of humanity and let suffering's color and texture transform within us. But we only do the amount of *Tonglen* that is manageable for us. We only take on what we can handle. And if the whole concept seems like too much, then we can do *Tonglen* in reverse.

Instead of breathing in discomfort, we breathe in contentment and ease, and let these comfortable feelings settle into us. As we breathe out, we send out the wish that others can be happy and feel this ease. We expand our consideration to all those around us who just want a break from their own suffering – large or small. With *Tonglen*, we transform the difficult and apply the easy, for the benefit of ourselves and others.

As we learn to make these transformations, we are empowered to address our own healing. But when it comes to self-healing, we may have received some confusing or frustrating advice. In a few self-help books, I read that I somehow participated in my own health issues through my own unconscious messages. I panicked. I didn't know how to undo these messages and I didn't want to carry such a big responsibility. How would I rewrite these messages? This was too much pressure. *Tonglen* helped me with this.

With *Tonglen* we can just rest in the notion that we are showing up and doing our bit. We can breathe in the emotions that we can deal with right now, and we can breathe out the relief we seek. No more guilt and no more worrying about how or if we contributed to our mental or physical health issues. We just deal with what is in front of us and find a way to bring ourselves some peace and quiet. Then healing occurs of its own accord, and those hidden messages, supposedly affecting our health, go through their own transformation unbeknownst to us. Soon we begin to feel shifts in our perceptions, and reactions, and physical well-being.

We all have the ability to absorb and transform. Every day, we remind ourselves that our house can hold anything, for it carries the strength and experience of lifetimes of knowing. In this next visualization, let this strength take you deep into your own understanding and wisdom.

Cave

As you turn your attention inward
Feel the sweet stillness of breath
And the quiet within the quiet
As you turn inward
Watch your body expand
And soften as you breathe
Profound and deep is your breath
Strong and flexible is your body

The depth of your breath
Alters your body
Allowing your arms to curve
Your belly to round
Into ancient walls of strength and history

Your body rounds into a deep and sacred cave
Pulling in all of your life
Your longing and your fear
Your body is able and willing

To hold its history
In this sacred bowl
Full of breath and quiet

You are this cave that is deep and forgiving
You are this body wrapping around itself
Curving in, retreating back, and then back again
Courageously and lovingly
Holding your ancestors close to your belly
You are the mother and the father
You are the children spilling out into the world
Outside you and around you
Are forms of chaos, excitement, and hope
But stillness keeps breathing you

You are retreating back, and then back again
Rounding and curving into this sacred bowl
Inside lives the stillness of stone
Where lights shimmer
And cool waters run
You don't mind, You don't move
Your roundness is gift enough

Thoughts and plans are no match for this quiet
You shelter them, but that is all
They cannot move your rock of stillness
They are not lucid enough to change your mind
Inside is where thoughts and beliefs
Have new life... breathed into them
As you round and curve and soften
Feel your breath take you deeper and deeper

Your body breathes with satisfaction
To be this vessel holding all of your life

Of everyone's life
As if the holding is your show of gratitude
To the stillness
And to the quiet
Within the quiet

In our own stillness, we learn to take on all kinds of emotions that we had previously avoided. Looking closely at what is right in front of us is now not so scary. We see our issues and remember that we are not alone – other people feel this. We are starting to focus on our similarities with others.

It's All in the Details

As we heard in Thich Nhat Hanh's boat story, we sometimes unconsciously adopt an *us and them* way of looking at the world. We feel separate from others, and often assume that only we feel this pain or discomfort. It is only *us* who are suffering. So we try to push ahead so we can triumph over *them*. Take driving in our cars for instance. If we are held up in traffic, and a car tries to inch ahead of us or cut us off, we perceive the other car as doing something to us. We might yell out, from the safety of our own seat, *What is that car doing? Move forward so I can get by! Does this person even know how to drive?* Then we finally have the chance to pass by the car and see who is driving. We see the person's face and they become real. Often we are a little surprised when we put a human face to the driver. Behind the wheel is an older gentleman looking lost, or a tired mom just trying to cope. Our anger changes in an instant.

In the details of the situation lies the compassion. The man's jacket reminds us of our late father's brown tweed coat that we just donated to charity. The mom's wet, curly hair suggests that she had only a window of time to shower before leaving the house. Hey, this feels like my life and everyone else's life. *Real* people are in all these cars. Who knew?

The details help us to see past *us and them*. If we enhance our view of the world with details, people come to life. Identification with our fellow humans replaces feelings of isolation and separation. In fact, molecular medicine tells us that we humans share *"all but 0.01% (1/100th of 1%) of identical genetic sequences."* So we are *"virtually identical to one another at the level of our genes (99.99%)."*[12]

The Obvious

When we are at odds with someone, we can always go back to a basic truth about us humans, and as obvious as this truth is, it is easily forgotten. No matter the age, the background or the personality, the person we are looking at is someone else's child. There was a mother who held this being and felt her heart melt. There was a father who looked to see how this child would fit into the world, or how they walked into a room, or how their bare feet looked on the kitchen floor. When we remember this truth, our conflict with a specific person can dissipate and we can see their humanity. Everyone around us is someone else's child.

Not So Scary

On this journey we start to be friendly with the idea of sitting still, staying with the feeling and facing whatever is arising. Sometimes facing what we are feeling can feel as easy as walking into water or as scary as walking into fire. We naturally gravitate to what we think is the easiest path. But sometimes the easiest path doesn't take us very far into the stillness we crave. Facing difficult emotions is scary and often avoided. But we toy with the idea of facing a little of what we normally would avoid. And, like facing any challenging situation or emotion, once you are in the middle of it, it disperses and loses its hold.

After awhile, we learn to move towards suffering rather than away from it because the rawness of the emotion can actually be a blessing. We can work with the bite of the emotion and transform it into relief by using its texture and shape to change our perceptions. We move towards what is, without shielding our eyes. We move towards the aching heart without covering our chest. Then we are free – not in spite of the suffering but in a way because of it. We learn to adjust to an uncomfortable moment by accepting it as it is and finding a way to be open, flexible and receptive. Becoming mindful of our present situation and accepting it as it is, is ultimately the means to seeing and feeling the possibility for peace in every moment. And our present situation can be as seemingly ordinary as a walk in the park, or as dramatic as life and death. In either case, we take in the details of the moment.

On the night my father died I was captured by only sound and light. The echo of the oxygen pump and the shadow of yellow light above his hospital bed defined the moment. I stood at the foot of his bed, my daughter sat by the window and we waited. That moment tasted of holding and releasing, of moisture and heat. That moment moved in and around us, brushed up against us, and then gathered us up in its silence.

I watched my father's eyes as they retreated. I held my father's hand and told him that I loved him, and realized that I was saying those words for the first time. That moment was the ultimate meditation for me. I was just there, allowing the presence to guide me, and allowing the moment to have its way.

Chapter Five

So Where Are We?

We are well on our way to creating a *practice* that can work for us. And we now know that meditation is not only for those people with good knees. Adapting and re-creating is how we make this journey come to life. We can apply what we know and what feels right in order to discover our own present moment. As our awareness increases, we start to see what is really going on with the mind. We've watched the comings and goings, we've stepped out of town for a while, and we've returned home. We've been inside rivers, up and down teeter-totters, and we have held a party for our friends. During all these journeys, our breath was a constant, even when we forgot that our breath was a constant.

Just by contemplating the ideas in this book, and by climbing into some of these waters, with your imagination in hand, your perceptions have started to shift. Perhaps unbeknownst to you, layers of compassion, tolerance and quiet reflection are now rising to the surface. Old habits that have been circling and circling the same old wagon have slowed down and started looking around. A pocket of lost air space has been spotted, if only for a split second. And this sighting constitutes a huge glimpse into a vast new stillness.

Whenever we are walking, sitting, lying or just living, we can step back or step in, or just watch. We have found our way into the delicious middle and now realize that perhaps location is only relative. In truth, we are in all places all the time. Thoughts are inside, outside, behind, in front of and around us all the time. And we are just here, creating our own experiences.

But creating our own experiences can be challenging. The

various ways that I have described this sweet and still air space may just be words to you – words, letters and shapes simply lying on the page, making no sense. Sometimes they make no sense to me. I will make notes about this great insight that I had during a meditation and then when I look at my notes later I think, *What? That isn't so profound.* So I close my eyes and go back in and try to recapture the idea, the vision, or the insight. Then I get it again, and a two-dimensional concept becomes a three-dimensional understanding.

Aligning yourself with stillness brings you into the ordinary in a new way. By showing up regularly in your boat, you are creating a foundation of stillness for daily life. You find that you are less reactive when your children are screaming. You feel calmer in stressful situations. Changes in schedules or plans don't throw you off. Daily activities just get easier.

Forgetting

Even after years of meditation, I forget to meditate. I forget that I have the ability to step back from, or step in to, or watch what is going on, because the pull of my busy mind is intoxicating and consuming. We all experience this. It is part of the human psyche, and we will probably be forgetting and then eventually remembering, for our whole lives. We forget that the thing we did last week with our breath felt gloriously restful. We forget that the visualization with the water, that we did yesterday, opened up an air space that felt primitive and deeply known. We forget to reach for meditation in order to get a break from busy-mind, and we forget that we didn't get a break. Thought trails and distracting emotions encourage us to check out and take a nap, and it seems to take forever for something or someone to come around and wake us up.

But now we can do the rousing for ourselves. Every day at some given time, we decide to show up and sit in our boat. We have just enough curiosity to want to see what will happen next.

The more we sit in the boat, the more we remember, and the more we remember the more we fortify our faith in the process.

Staying With It

So we go back to the boat, and back to the breath, and back to watching thoughts over and over again. Repetition is okay. It doesn't mean we're dense; it just means we're human. In fact, repetition helps embed new sensations and experiences. So, we forget and then we remember; always returning to our focus. Every time we return, we get another chance to experience something new; to find a profound stillness that we sort of knew was there all along.

When we commit to something – even if we are a little haphazard about it – the unexpected starts to happen. New feelings and perceptions appear out of nowhere. When we think of an endeavor or sport or project that we donated a lot of our time to, we recall that the love or drive, that kept us showing up, produced some interesting results. We could see or feel improvement or change. Consistency allows for transformation.

As you stay with it, you apply gentle determination. Finding a way to focus without force is the trick. You will learn to feel the subtle difference between pushing in order to focus and releasing in order to focus. Remember that this difference is separated by a thin veil that billows and swells with your positioning. To know which side of the veil you are on is your mission. At any moment, you can exhale and change sides. And as you change your position and move into what frees you, you fall away from what holds you. The falling away is the unhinging and releasing into that lost air space.

As always, when we begin to experience shifts – big or small – we do so with an open mind. Each time we meditate we could experience a different shift. We really don't know how each meditation will look. The meditation journey is unpredictable. If we try for the same incredible opening we had before, we may fall short. So we stay open to whatever happens. If we don't expect an ideal state to emerge from meditation but can just *be with* where we are, then we can relax with the whole thing.

Customizing

Each time you approach meditation, ask yourself how the journey will look today. A specific method or image that helped you yesterday may not work today. You might be confused because this method always worked before, exactly as it was, but now it feels forced and restrictive. So you move on and change the method. You can ask yourself, *What is true today? What is distracting me now? What might work today?* Then you get creative. You take the absolute conviction that you have the ability to design a meditation that can serve you, and you get creative. Methods come in all shapes and sizes. For example, for many years I was consumed with the work thoughts that I took home from the office. These thoughts were too strong to step back from. Stepping back would just produce tension. What I really wanted was to just step *away* from them or have them vanish.

However, I knew that I just needed to create a new image and method that could allow me to stay with the work thoughts. Then I could accept them in a different way – without just *pretending* that I was accepting them. The need to create a new image and method is accompanied by the willingness to let the old stuff go. I let go of this one, then I let go of that one, over and over again to see what was right for the moment.

Letting go meant keeping my mind from getting too involved. I needed to watch and wait for a new image to be born in and of itself. I realized that it was best to go with the first image that appeared. For work thoughts I would often reinvent the side-by-side image that we saw in *Stepping Back*. I wanted to keep work thoughts sitting benignly beside me, but not strangling me. Here is where true awareness comes in. We need to have our radar highly tuned in order to detect whether we are covering up or sitting with. We are learning to feel the almost imperceptible difference between the two.

Flexibility and creativity will serve you well. You can take the structure laid out in this book as it is, or shape it into a system that works for you. Try the various metaphors and images, and see if they fit your style. Use whatever you can and leave the rest. Everyone's journey will look a little different. But by showing up on a regular basis, you will find a joy that runs deeper in your being than you thought possible.

Running Deep

I believe in the basic goodness of all beings. Once we strip away our rough outer edges, which have been strengthened by our human tendency to grasp and cling, we find the seeds of virtue and benevolence. We are learning to shed the habits and trappings which make us unhappy, and which mask our basic kindness and grace. Stepping back facilitates this shedding by allowing us to unfasten, to release and to fall away.

Through meditation, we are free to experience the full and rich feeling of nothingness. Here, I am referring to the interesting side of nothingness, the ineffable side that is everything and nothing at the same time. Now this is probably the most difficult concept to put into words, but as you do this *meditation thing* you will eventually say, *"Oh, I see what that means."* A generous trust in the process will take you far.

In this ocean of emptiness and quiet, we gather wisdom and clarity, which accompany us on our journey back in. We step into our town and into ourselves where we can sit deeply in our seat, not disturbed or thrown off, just sitting and being. This sounds like a tall order but actually it is quite possible. This newly found air space is closer than you think. You can often find it at the very end of any exhalation. You follow the line that the out-breath rides on, and at the very tip of this line, before you inhale, are stillness and space.

Some may say that all of this sounds too good to be true. That the idea of unlimited expansion means we are opening up a cavern of what seems like unbearable space. Is it unbearable or is it something we *can* bear? Can we experience an expansion in all directions allowing our old fearful self to seep out, leaving a huge amount of openness? We'll see.

We step in with bravery and curiosity, and the understanding that emotions will rise and fall, fears will come and go, and hidden joys will suddenly appear. Some days, it will all seem like too much. So you pace yourself and decide not to force the process. Your knowing is patient and wise and will take you where you need to go, one step at a time. As the German poet Rilke says, *"Let everything happen to you, beauty and terror, just keep going, no feeling is final."*[13]

Bud and all of us can create bigger pauses in our lives. The quiet between our words and our thoughts will tingle with newness, yet resonate with ancient memory. We will pull the silences from the corners of the room, and invite them in for tea. The sacred part of everyday life will begin to show itself. Our mission here is small, beautiful and simple. It is as easy as taking our next breath.

Reference Guide

For your easy reference, I am listing, by chapter, the various meditation exercises found in the book. However, I use the word exercise with caution. Remember to think of the exercises as experiments. You are the curious scientist who is exploring what can and cannot work for you, for the purpose of discovering something unknown. If one exercise doesn't seem to be working for today, come back to it tomorrow.

Watching Meditations

Watching the Breath
Page 11
Remember that when you start watching the breath, you ignore the voice that says, *been there, done that*. The key sensations to note are how air moves in and out of your body, and how your body moves as you breathe. Notice what expands and what doesn't expand. Notice how breath feels and sounds within you. If you lose focus, notice how quickly thoughts come in. See if you can count the number of thoughts you have in a ten-second period. You are simply taking stock.

Pretending
Page 12
This is where you bring out your inner actor. You will be *pretending* that staying focused on the breath is easy – as though we have been doing this kind of focusing forever. *Pretend* that you can easily focus on your breathe and body. *Pretend* that you can feel and hear air moving through you as you breathe in and out. This simple pretending can actually alter your experience.

Dissection
Page 13
By dissecting what is happening with your busy mind, you can unhinge from endless thought trails. You will be looking directly at your mind's activities. You will be naming and writing down the thoughts that distract you, and noticing the patterns, associations, strengths and weaknesses of your thoughts. You can name everything that you feel, sense, smell, taste, think and worry about. Then as the witness, you begin the process of differentiating yourself from the endless trails of thoughts.

Derailment
Page 15
This is an exercise to increase your awareness of the first thought that takes you away from your focus. You will notice whether it is an idea or sound that initially distracts you. Then you will notice the trail of thoughts that completely derail you. You will learn to incorporate the distracting sound or idea into your focus on the breath. You can transform the derailment by letting the distraction become part of the process of watching and breathing.

Looping Back
Page 16
This exercise helps you see how an initial distraction, whether sound or belief, encourages a leap to the next distraction which leads to the next, and so on. You will then stop the mind from wandering after perhaps four or five leaps, and loop back to the first thought that took you away. You trace backwards in order to identify the initial distraction. Familiarity with the first thought leap helps you catch your distractions more easily, and ultimately gives you more focused time with the breath.

Push Versus No Push
Page 19
With this exercise you will train yourself to be very highly tuned to the sensations of pushing and not pushing. By practicing with your hand on a pillow or by focusing on an object, you will feel the subtleties of effort and non-effort. Through keen detection, you will reinforce your perception of the subtle difference between tension and non-tension. Feeling the slight nuances of breathing, pushing, non-pushing and watching will take you far. The more you can recognize pushing, the less it actually occurs.

Holding On
Page 20
Your *shenpa* is your level of holding on or reaction to a particular thought, idea or situation. When you work with *shenpa* you begin to develop some very healthy neutrality as your mind eases up on its strong identification with notions, ideas or situations. In this exercise, you will be writing down the level of *shenpa* you have with your various thoughts. You can rate them one way, strong or weak, and then you can reverse the rating and see what happens.

I'd Rather Be
Page 25
You can make clear decisions that affect the nature of your meditations. With this exercise, you will see how the simple phrase, *I'd rather be,* holds enough conviction to easily bring you back to a quiet focus. You will be trying out, *I'd rather be connected to breath,* or *I'd rather be feeling quiet,* or *I'd rather be experiencing more room in my head,* or *I'd rather be with what is.* You will learn that your experience of your mind is wide open to very creative play.

Tapping
Page 32

In this exercise, you use the physical reminder of tapping on the body to help keep you focused, and to help you place the breath in the body. You will be gently tapping, at various intervals, on different parts of your body. You will use sensations from the tapping as the key reminders to come back to the breath, allowing the mind engagement to be minimal and constructive. The tapping exercise will help you become mindful of where your body and breath are, and will help curtail the endless thought trails.

Drinking Water
Page 34

Sipping on a glass of water can also teach you about the endless possibilities of the meditation experience. The key sensations to focus on are the sense of cool liquid entering your body, and the feeling of the water winding its way deep into your body. If your mind comes in and says, *I am just drinking water, no big deal*, just go back to the physical sensations. You want your mind to lose itself along the thread of cool water. After awhile, your mind will flip over into only sensing, and flip out of cognitive awareness of the process of drinking.

Other Anchors
Page 35

You can use other physical anchors to feel the depth of your breath and your awareness of thought. With the small pillow, you will follow the up and down movement of breath in your chest. Just as you did when drinking water, you can take note of the flip away from mind and into sensation. The flip indicates the movement out of form and into free air space. You will begin to develop your own images and metaphors that take you beyond the mind's questions and analyzing. Your body/breath team will come up with its own creative way into the air space. Being fluid with your techniques will keep you open-minded, flexible and curious.

Stepping Back Meditations

Time to Step
Page 46
This will be your first step back. You will use your breath to take your imaginary and barely perceptible step. Try to personalize the concept of stepping back so it becomes something that feels right to you. In so doing, you create a very subtle and slight separation between you as the watcher and you as the busy mind. You can use the thin veil imagery to understand the close proximity between the witness and the busy thoughts, as you step back and forth between the two.

Noticing
Page 46
As you practice stepping back, you will be noticing the subtle difference between holding and releasing, between tension and ease, and between thought and no thought. You will notice the feeling of trying to make the meditation work, and then the feeling of not trying. It will help to say to yourself, *I am aware that I have many thoughts. I am aware that I am breathing* and *I am aware that I am stepping back.* You will go back and forth between working at it, and not working at it. As you alternate between these two positions, you will notice that trying feels like thinking, and that not trying feels like releasing.

Picturing It
Page 48
In this exercise, you will create your own image of the location into which you are stepping back. You will create a vivid image

of this location using color and texture. When you have a clear picture of the location, you will easily step back into it, allowing yourself to unhinge from demanding thoughts. You will be sensing the differentiation between thought in the old location, and non-thought in the new location. An endless trial of demanding thoughts will try to get your attention. You will simply notice them and step back again. You will be noticing and stepping back over and over again. Knowledge of your mind's activities will lead to very clear insights.

Shadowing
Page 56
Shadowing is an exercise that keeps you meditating even when you aren't officially meditating. You will learn to move through your day or a specific task with a meditative stillness accompanying you. The busy-mind-you will be shadowed by the empty-quiet-you. Your deep core of stillness is your essential nature and it is always with you. With shadowing, you will begin to notice that you can be in chaos while still in quiet. You will become aware that there is an essence of your being that is always anchored in presence. Shadowing will help you to recognize the continuum from meditation to daily life.

Amnesia
Page 57
To counter the occurrence of meditation amnesia, you will learn two handy tips to bring your awareness back to the breath and the present moment. First, you will be imagining a thin thread of awareness that leads you back to the moment. As you are led back, you allow the thread to transform into breath. You repeatedly remind yourself that your thread of breath is a constant, with tremendous memory. Secondly, you will be picking a word that brings back the memory of the air space where breath and the present moment live. You will use the first

word that comes to mind and repeat it to yourself throughout the day. Your word can be different each day or can be a word that stays with you for a while.

Reversing Our Thinking
Page 60
In this exercise, you will learn to change how you perceive your thoughts, which will change your experience. You will be bringing out your inner actor again and pretending that you can't hold on to your thoughts. You will see them slipping through your fingers like water in the hand. You can imagine that you can't hold on to them. When your mind comes in and says, *This is silly* or *This won't work*, you simply acknowledge these comments and keep going. You act your way to a freedom from invasive thought patterns.

In the Body
Page 68
This is a simple sensing exercise that combines watching the breath with stepping back. You will be following the rhythm of your breath and stepping back as you exhale. This focus on breath diverts the mind's attention to the body, where it needs to be. Sensing moving air in the body is a key way to shift out of busy-mind, and to enhance your ability to step back from your busy mind. When you tap into the body presence, you recognize the simplicity of a life without excessive thinking.

Unhinging
Page 69
Just as Ann did when she felt enormous fear arising, you can displace and unhinge from fear, or any other strong emotion, on to a piece of paper. You will be drawing a stick figure of yourself, and then drawing the location of the fear. Then you will create an image of yourself stepping back from the drawing into an air

space of stillness. Each time the fear starts to follow you into this air space, you will unhinge by taking another step back and differentiating yourself from the emotion lying on the paper.

Apart From Pain
Page 71

This two-part drawing exercise will help you to get some distance from physical pain. First, you will be drawing a stick figure of yourself and then drawing the location of a somewhat manageable pain. You will then be moving the drawing away from you, in order to feel a psychological separation between yourself and the pain. Secondly, you will be drawing the location of a bigger and more distracting pain, and then highlighting the outer edge of the image ball with a different colored pen. Then you will pour imaginary water over the pain image and watch how the colorful outer edge of the pain image begins to soften and melt. With the power of your imagination, you can transform the nature, form and strength of pain.

Displacing
Page 73

Here you can use the image of one object displacing another in water, in order to experience the unhinging of sticky thoughts. With the concept of displacement in mind, you will imagine the smooth and liquid separation of particles of thoughts from your core self. Remember that your core self has the wisdom to make this differentiation, and the ability to step back from the endless stream of thoughts and reactions. Displacement occurs in the body, and you settle into sweet relief.

Fixed Emotions
Page 74

In this exercise, you will work with an intense emotion with which you have been struggling. You will assign imagery to this emotion in three ways. First, using the theory that you are over 50 percent water, you imagine the emotion moving freely within your body. Secondly you will imagine pouring water over the emotion and then watching the emotion's outer shell soften, as bits and pieces begin to fall away. And finally, you will become the water that is pouring over the emotion. By changing your mind about challenging emotions you assist in the shifting and unhinging of seemingly solid and tenacious forms. You can find breathing space and welcome relief where you may have thought there was none.

Stepping In Meditations

Using Whatever We Have
Page 83
With this exercise you will use consistent sound or white noise to take you deeper into meditation. You will imagine the sound as a wave with a particular size and shape, and you will watch how the sound wave enters your body. You will learn to reverse your thinking about how a sound affects you, by climbing inside the sound and seeing what is there for you to use. You will imagine or pretend that the power of the sound wave can create some space in you, and that your breath can widen into this new space. As you settle into this new space, you will hear the present moment.

Using Other Sounds
Page 85
Here you will be experimenting with intermittent noises that are part of your everyday life. You will be calling upon your creative forces to transform the way you experience lawnmowers or barking dogs or any other sound that could distract you from your meditation. Once you identify the texture or sensation of a sound, you will be able to incorporate the sound into your

practice. In so doing, you become more tolerant of your environment, and realize that you can meditate anywhere.

Toning
Page 89
You will be creating a sound or tone that can help you deal with pain, tightness or constriction. You want to allow for long, easy and breathy sounds. The breathy sound will turn into a long comfortable tone that will represent relief, as it winds its way through any constriction. Experiment with the length and texture of the tone. You will be creating some room, some breathing space inside of pain. In this way, you will be moving with pain rather than pushing against it.

Moving Around
Page 97
This is a new take on the traditional walking meditation. You will be sensing and taking note of the various textures, temperatures and shapes of the objects you come in contact with. Your hands will interpret densities and properties. Your mind will take note of the essential fluid nature of the objects and beings it is seeing. This moving meditation can travel with you throughout your day. As you move, remember the imagery of molecules and particles that make up all living forms.

A Closer Look
Page 98
With this exercise, you will be studying the various densities of thoughts, and then winding a thread of breath through these densities. You will understand that just as matter can be dense and thick, or light and airy so, too, can your thoughts. You will notice that your thread of breath changes its form and shape from day to day or from situation to situation to conform to the density of your thoughts. This exercise will show you that your

thought patterns are not fixed dense matter, and that you can use the flexibility and adaptability of the breath to find the space within the matter.

Down Through the Feet
Page 100
This stepping meditation is a virtual walking meditation that allows you to map out your route ahead of time. The key sensation to notice is the sense of your real feet sliding into the footprints laid out by your virtual feet, or your cloth feet that you have cut out in the shape of your footprint. As each real step meets its virtual step or its cloth step you become very anchored in that walking moment. You are reinforcing the feeling of complete presence in your stepping meditation.

Doing the Opposite
Page 102
Although the practice of *Tonglen* seems counterintuitive, we can try this practice in order to increase compassion for ourselves and for those around us. With *Tonglen* you breathe in everything that frightens or worries you and you breathe out relief. Try *Tonglen* as an experiment in doing something completely counterintuitive. You can start by doing *Tonglen* for yourself, using your breath as the means to breathe in an emotion and transform it into relief. You will see how a particular emotion can dissipate and lose its charge. When you try *Tonglen* for others, remember that the other people feel the same emotions or discomfort that you do. You can use your breath and your intention to make these transformations.

Notes

1. Pema Chodron – *Bodhisattva Mind* (Sounds True, 2006)
2. Pema Chodron – *Getting Unstuck: The Habit of Distraction* (Sounds True, 2005)
3. www.positive-personal-growth.com/what-does-love mean.html
4. Eckart Tolle – *Stillness Speaks* (New World Library and Namaste Publishing, 2003)
5. Thich Nhat Hanh – *Looking Deeply: Mindfulness and Meditation – Classic Dharma Talks* (Parallax Press, 2002)
6. http://www.sciencedaily.com/releases/2009/02/090203110514.htm
7. http://www.physorg.com/news177058708.html
8. Joni Mitchell – *People's Parties* (Crazy Crow Music ©, 1973)
9. http://www.physorg.com/news10312.html
10. Jill Bolte Taylor, Ph.D. – *My Stroke of Insight* (Penguin Books, 2006)
11. Pema Chodron – *Good Medicine* (Sounds True, 2001)
12. Jill Bolte Taylor, Ph.D. – *My Stroke of Insight* (Penguin Books, 2006)
13. Rainer Maria Rilke – *Book of Hours: Love Poems to God* – translated by Anita Burrows and Joanna Macy (Penguin Group, 1996)

BOOKS

O is a symbol of the world, of oneness and unity. In different cultures it also means the "eye," symbolizing knowledge and insight. We aim to publish books that are accessible, constructive and that challenge accepted opinion, both that of academia and the "moral majority."

Our books are available in all good English language bookstores worldwide. If you don't see the book on the shelves ask the bookstore to order it for you, quoting the ISBN number and title. Alternatively you can order online (all major online retail sites carry our titles) or contact the distributor in the relevant country, listed on the copyright page.

See our website www.o-books.net for a full list of over 500 titles, growing by 100 a year.

And tune in to myspiritradio.com for our book review radio show, hosted by June-Elleni Laine, where you can listen to the authors discussing their books.

MySpiritRadio